A HISTORY OF SURF CULTURE

Surfers are members of a different race of people
from the man in the street.

Nat Young, *1966 World Surfing Champion*

A HISTORY OF SURF CULTURE

Drew Kampion   Bruce Brown

EVERGREEN

Frontcover: Laird Hamilton in the straps at Jaws.
Backcover: Tom Blake and Duke Kahanamoku, about 1935.

EVERGREEN is an imprint of TASCHEN GmbH

© for this edition: 2003 TASCHEN GmbH
Hohenzollernring 53, D–50672 Köln
www.taschen.com
First published
by General Publishing Group, Inc.
Los Angeles
Copyright © 1997 by Drew Kampion
Cover design: Catinka Keul, Cologne

Printed in Spain
ISBN 3–8228–3000–3

For John Severson, who started it all.

CONTENTS

FOREWORD 21

INTRODUCTION 23

THE SEED CULTURE 29

THE BOOM CULTURE 73

FROM SOUL TO PRO 125

CONTEMPORARY CORE 175

ACKNOWLEDGEMENTS 210

BIBLIOGRAPHY 211

CREDITS 212

INDEX 214

FOREWORD

A book on "surf culture" – WOW! We were always told we were a bunch of "uncultured" BOZOS! Back in the early '50s, when I started surfing, the main comment from parents and non-surfing peers was: "When you grow up, you'll realize you were wasting your time when you could have been doing something useful."

I could never figure out why golf, tennis, baseball, football or being a cheerleader was "useful" and surfing wasn't. Then the Hollywood beach movies came and that didn't help us out. They just confirmed what most people thought anyway – a bunch of surfers having food fights and drooling. Actually, we did have food fights, but we didn't drool.

I always loved the ocean and surfing and couldn't understand why everyone didn't share my views. I figured everyone would rather live in an expando trailer next to a perfect point break with no one around, than in a mansion in Beverly Hills.

I ran into a guy the other day who was rounding up some cattle. He said, "I used to be a surfer when I was a kid, but when I grew up I became a cowboy."

"That's funny," I said. "When I was a kid, I was a cowboy, but when I grew up I became a surfer." He didn't get it.

The young cinematographer in search of the perfect wave.

What became a "lifestyle" later was just how we lived without giving it much thought. We knew we had to live by the ocean and needed to figure out a way to make a living there. Hobie made surfboards, Gordon Clark made foam blanks, John Severson started Surfer magazine, I started making movies. Some guys became firemen (time off), some became teachers (time off).

Whatever we did, the main focus was how it would affect our surf time. Getting rich wasn't important. What was important was having the freedom to do what we wanted. It didn't mean we didn't take our jobs or professions seriously; we did. It meant keeping things in perspective. After the release of *The Endless Summer*, people in the movie business would tell me, if I wanted to be successful in the motion picture industry, I would have to move to Hollywood. I said I would rather be a milkman at the beach than live in Hollywood. I wasn't kidding then, and I'm still not kidding now.

If you gave most "true" surfers the choice of moving to New York and working at an ad agency in Manhattan and making a ton of money or staying at the beach and "getting by," the vote would be: the beach. I guess all this stuff is "lifestyle," but it takes someone like Drew to point it out to me.

I guess my answer to the question we were asked as kids – When are you going to grow up? – is, I hope, never.

Bruce Brown, *Gaviota*, California. July 1997

INTRODUCTION

Like thousands of surfers over the past 50 years, I rode my first wave at Malibu. At the time, I felt my first awkward ride on a small wall of surging whitewater was my rite of passage, my initiation, into a new world. In reality, it was merely the first step into a subculture built around continual initiation.

Subculture. My big, fat Random House dictionary describes it as "a group having social, economic, ethnic, or other traits distinctive enough to distinguish it from others within the same culture or society." *A cult?* "A group having a sacred ideology and a set of rites centering around their sacred symbols." Surfing, I would discover, was the subcult of stoked.

As a teenager living in the San Fernando Valley on the outskirts of Los Angeles, I was superficially aware of two significant sub-cultures: the greasers and the surfers. One had black, oiled hair and glowered, the other was bleach blond with a dopey smile. Neither was especially appealing, but of course both of them were. Were it not for a girlfriend's determination to go off by herself and learn to surf, I might never have purchased my first surfboard (a 9'6" Roberts that had been broken almost exactly in half and glassed back together) for $50 in the summer of '62. Unconsciously, in making a commitment to attempt this new sport, I had taken a step toward membership in this crude and shallow culture. My perception changed after I rode my first wave of whitewater late one afternoon.

It had taken me weeks of effort and embarrassment (I was no natural athlete) and now, finally, standing on my board, being pushed smoothly and steadily toward the Malibu sands by a modest surge of whitewater, I was suspended in a corona of absolute bliss. I don't know what else to call it. I was so incredibly stoked and so utterly alive! I was riding an ocean wave. I was surfing!

Many others caught their first wave that summer of '62. In fact, I was a child of the early '60s surfing baby boom, an influx that so disgusted and oppressed the wave-riders who'd always had the beaches to themselves that some of them gave it up with a groan or hit the road, becoming global coastal predators forever on the hunt for perfect uncrowded waves.

OPPOSITE: **Waves sweeping silently toward Sunset Beach during a big winter swell in December 1974.**

ABOVE: **The author in Puerto Rico "covering" the 1968 World Contest.**

As it happened, I was getting into surfing precisely at a significant point of transition in the sport and subculture – the passage from the era of the "seed" culture to the era of "pop" or "fad" culture. It was an extraordinary moment, really. Here was a sport that had been created more than a thousand years ago by a people living in an earthly paradise, a sport that was pulled back from the brink of extinction and oblivion by a joint effort of *kama'aina* and *haole* believers. Now, just as I was beginning to taste it, this same culture was suddenly the subject of a new American fad. The beach, that outlaw zone, was becoming very popular. All of that essence we had inherited, all of that long and hard-earned culture, was being swallowed up in the stampede to the beach. The heart of surfing was being devoured.

The new popularity of the sport created new pressures. Waves that had always been plentiful were now growing scarce, like a banquet to which too many guests had been invited. Surfing is not like football or baseball. You don't fence off Malibu and say that only the pros can surf here now, and you can't charge $100 to surf 18 waves (not yet anyway). In surfing, surfers of all skill levels, ages, sizes and philosophies must share the water and vie for the waves.

See-through Pipeline – food for stoke!

OPPOSITE: **Drew Kampion at *Surfer* in 1969.**

The pecking order was pretty wicked at Malibu in those days. The guys who had had it to themselves in the '50s were still there whenever the waves were good – Mickey Dora, Dewey Weber, Lance Carson, "Tubesteak" Tracey, "Cowboy" Henderson, Johnny Fain and a few dozen other very good surfers. Then there were the beginners – the kooks – like me. Getting good waves to ride at the premier south-swell spot on the Southern California coast was largely a matter of luck. I didn't do too well those first couple of years.

Nursed on leftover waves in crowded summer playpens, I was jazzed by euphoric Beach Boys sounds, whipped into a frenzy by the surf movies of the time (both the esoteric four-wall surf films and the major Hollywood sludge that so totally misrepresented anything whatsoever remotely true about my surfing experience) and stirred to poetic appreciations and longings by the equanimity and gelatinous perfection of California summertime waves.

I stood in line with the throngs on a perfect spring afternoon outside the Santa Monica Civic Auditorium beneath the marquee that read, *The Endless Summer*. And when Terrence led Mike Hynson and Robert August over the dunes to Cape St. Francis, and I beheld the most perfect waves I'd ever seen, I could taste them, and, I admit it, I lusted in my heart of hearts for a go at "Bruce's beauties." I was insatiably stoked.

Even today, after 35 years of surfing, the smell of warm neoprene and a good sniff of a bar of coconut surf wax are all the aromatherapy I need to get focused and back in perspective. I remain thoroughly stoked.

Surfing has undergone enormous changes since I rode my first waves at Malibu. Millions of people now surf worldwide, a large percentage of them in places that were unknown to surfers back in the early '60s. Surfboards have steadily evolved over those 35-plus years, and equipment has always had an enormous influence on the direction of the sport. The level of performance has gone through the roof. The gymnastic contortions of today's radical surfers would have been unimaginable in 1960, let alone in 1900. Surfers spend almost as much time flying through the air nowadays as they do carving across the water. Bigger waves are being ridden than ever thought possible. In many ways, surfing has become an "extreme sport," in turn stimulating other extreme sports.

At the same time, a living archeology is evident. The ancient *wiliwili* tree grows out a layer at a time, and when you cut it down to make your surfboard, all the rings are there, from the first year to the last. So it is with surfing. You can see it out in the water and on the beach at many of the popular surf spots today – long boards and short boards, young kids and old farts, longhairs and burrheads, laid-back styles of the '30s and aggressive rip-and-tear styles of the '90s.

Some surfers paddle out into the water carrying with them an enormous sense of the sport's history. They have a sense of time, an appreciation of the elemental beauty of their encounter with the waves. They know they stand at the top of a ladder that has been built over generations, but that the essential reality remains the same: man and wave.

Other surfers see it as just something they gotta do, something all their friends do, something cool, something rad, something totally wild and "sick" (meaning, as we said in olden times, "hairball"), something out of bounds to move the schoolday/workday lymph out of their brains. Surfing is escape into the pure now of it!

Luckily, this strange and magical sport is a big container. It can be almost anything to almost anyone. And the energy just keeps on coming. Every new wave is like peeling up the sheet on an Etch-a-Sketch™ and starting a new game, or a new work of art, or just, well, a new sketch.

The surf culture that has formed concentric rings around the elemental act of riding a wave is a unique and strangely powerful phenomenon. It is a subculture that feeds on the experiences and truths gained in the ocean and on the waves, and it is a subculture that has enormous effects on the larger cultures of which it is a part.

Surf culture is quite a bit like a Trojan horse. Its outward form – its energy and essential eroticism (what better natural metaphor for sex?) – makes it appealing and charismatic. Everyone wants a piece of it; it's cool to be associated with it; it's got the sizzle that makes the sell. But something else, something very ancient and esoteric, comes along with it, and when that gets loose in the culture at large, well, anything can happen. Things change. That old Polynesian seed starts to work its way into the rigid Northern cultural soul and – *bam!* – suddenly people are stoked!

This book is offered to surfers as a reminder of who we are, where we come from and how fundamentally important it is to ride waves. For nonsurfers, those who surfing great Phil Edwards once referred to as "the Legions of the Unjazzed," this book is a window into a world without boundaries – a world fed by a renewable energy resource that charges its inhabitants with a fire to continually push their limitations in pursuit of ever-higher levels of stoke.

Drew Kampion, *Whidbey Island*, Washington. June 1, 1997

The Essence of Surfing

Surfing is the deceptively simple act of riding a breaking ocean wave on a surfboard. In reality, as a fundamental physical feat, surfing on a wave is a phenomenal conjunction of forces; the mathematics of it are profoundly complex. However, as an expression of the essential relationship between man and nature, surfing is unique in its clarity. And as a metaphor for life and just about anything life throws at us, it is unparalleled. Life is a wave. Albert Einstein even said so.

Everything in the material world manifests itself in waves, but while the dynamics of waves modulate all phases of our existence, nowhere is this fact more graphically apparent than when man goes to sea. The most archetypal and symbolic representation of this relationship – between man and the rhythms and power of nature – is expressed in the act of riding a wave. The elemental purity of this encounter goes a long way in explaining surfing's almost universal appeal.

The essence of perfection: The surfer is about to be wrapped in a clean dry barrel. Burleigh Head, Queensland, Australia.

ABOVE: The essence of the search: Kevin Naughton finds what he's looking for off Tavarua Island, Fiji.

THE SEED CULTURE

"Go strip off your clothes that are a nuisance in this mellow clime. Get in and wrestle with the sea; wing your heels with the skill and power that reside in you, hit the sea's breakers, master them, and ride upon their backs as a king should." Jack London, *The Cruise of the Snark,* 1911

Out of the south they came, paddling their large voyaging canoes – twin-hulled vessels equipped with sails of woven pandanus leaves. They carried men, women and children, and as many provisions as would fit into the boats. They paddled north out of the waters of their Polynesian home and far into the unknown regions, creeping across the gigantic equatorial water-plain with no sure knowledge of where they were going or what they would find. When their hopes dimmed and they contemplated retreat, legend says a huge white shark appeared and began to lead them.

The most astute pilots the world has ever known, these Polynesians navigated by stars and wind and clouds, and by the patterns that wind and land and currents create on the water. The keen observer can detect the residue of a swell's encounter with an island many miles away, and somewhere, a thousand nautical miles above the equator, the navigators began to detect signs of land. According to legend, that first weary but resolved flotilla came out of the vast near-infinite wilderness of the south to touch land directly on the southernmost tip of the southernmost island of the Hawai'ian archipelago, the most remote islands on earth.

The Polynesian relationship to the sea was unlike anything the Europeans experienced. To the islanders, the ocean meant life and joy and freedom. This photo of a lone surfer with his short paipo board at Waikiki in the 1890s speaks volumes. But by 1900, disease, religion and a new industrial work ethic had all but exterminated Hawai'ian culture and the ancient sport of surfing.

OPPOSITE: The stoke of surfing was at the heart of the ancient Hawai'ian culture.

SURFING IN PARADISE

The cult of surf was born in some irretrievably distant past – nobody knows where or how for certain. Certainly, the first people who went out onto the ocean in boats quickly became aware of the inherent capacity of waves to either propel or oppose a craft. Perhaps the answer is woven into the DNA of coastal dwellers in West Africa or in Peru, where the two greatest natural powers worshipped were rainbows and waves. Certainly, it is deeply seated in the essence of the Hawai'ian culture.

Olo and Alaia

The construction of the surfboard was an important part of early surf culture. There were two kinds of boards – the *olo*, used only by the chiefs and made from the *wiliwili* tree, and the *alaia*, used by the common people and made of *koa*. When building their boards, the early Hawai'ians performed numerous rituals. When a tree was selected, a red *kuma* fish was placed at its trunk as an offering of payment. A prayer was then said before cutting it down. The fallen tree was then cut to the surfboard's rough dimensions using a stone adze and hauled down to the canoe house for the final shaping with coral and rough stone. Before the board was used, other rites and ceremonies were performed for its dedication.

Hawai'ian myth and legend abound with tales of great adventures in the surf, and the first Europeans to see this incredible sport marvelled at the islanders' prowess and tried to capture the complex mechanics in idealized illustrations.

OPPOSITE: **Surfboards were valued possessions and carefully maintained.**

The Hawai'ian Islands are the consummate earthly paradise. Rising tall and green above white sand beaches out of a warm turquoise sea, the still-living volcanic islands were sublime, powerful, iconic, dramatic and without a living human soul when the first adventurous settlers from the south arrived. Their great heights and archetypal monolithic rock formations, the living pits of roiling lava, the ever-present rhythmic crashing of the sea all around, the alternating breath of tradewinds, Kona storms and hurricanes all yielded the subconscious images fundamental to the development of a great cultural mythology.

There is ample evidence of surfboard riding throughout the South Pacific before contact with the Europeans, but nowhere was it so significant to the culture as in Hawai'i. This may have been because of the sheer quantity and quality of the waves in the Hawai'ian Islands, which are situated dead center in the largest body of water on the planet, leaving it perfectly exposed to waves from all directions. Logistically and architecturally, the islands were created for surfing!

Perhaps the Polynesians who ventured so far north on their voyages of discovery were surfers who left the south in search of a fabled chain of beautiful islands with perfect waves. Whatever prompted their search, once in Hawai'i, the party of explorers flourished into a new civilization. With roots steeped in traditional Polynesian values, the new culture adapted its mythology and lifestyle to these northern islands, especially in developing new ways of riding and playing in the ocean waves. As far as we know, this was the first real surf culture.

"Surf riding was one of the favorite Hawaiian sports," wrote Thomas G. Thrum in his 1896 *Hawaiian Almanac and Annual*, one of the best surviving sources of information on surfboard riding and its place at the core of ancient Hawai'ian culture. Chiefs, men, women and youth all participated, and the daily chores were put aside whenever a good surf was running. The islands' royalty especially loved riding the waves and gave themselves the privilege of reserving the better surf spots for their use alone.

The Hawai'ian people were deeply entrenched in their surfing and the powerful energy of the vast ocean that surrounded them. They had almost as many names for the types of waves and breakers as Eskimos have for snow. During prolonged flat spells, the ocean was ritually beaten with kelp and chanted to in order to "coax" up a swell.

Even as late as the second half of the 18th century, it remained clear that the pre-contact Hawai'ians were expert surfers. They crafted their surfboards in ways that revealed their spiritual consciousness and profound understanding of wave mechanics as well as their serious appetite for having fun in the surf. Like a tree, the strength of these ancient Polynesian roots continues to be the source of life in modern surf culture. Certainly, the few rare 200-year-old surfboards held in sanctuary at Honolulu's Bishop Museum are scarcely able to suggest what went on over the centuries before Captain James Cook's two-ship fleet, HMS *Resolution* and HMS *Discovery*, sighted the islands in 1778.

Captain James Cook

The first island sighted by Cook and the crew of *Resolution* at dawn on January 18, 1778, was O'ahu. Shortly thereafter, they spotted Kaua'i, then Niihau. They were at the northwest end of the Hawai'ian archipelago canvassing the North Pacific for islands while waiting for the return of summer to head back to the North American

two ships were halted by a gleaming wall of ice. Cook decided to return to winter on the islands he'd named Sandwich after his patron back at the Admiralty. Approaching the islands from the east this time, he struck Maui first, and when the natives paddled out, some had already been infected with venereal disease – three large

and so smoothly by the sea." But even this energetic preview did little to prepare Cook and crew for Hawai'i. The sight of natives riding waves on specially crafted pieces of wood was like seeing aliens walking upside down in trees.

Cook's round-the-world expedition was his third on behalf of the British Royal Navy, but not

continent in search of the Northwest Passage. When a few brown-skinned natives ventured out in canoes to see what these strange floating birds were, Cook was surprised and delighted to hear a dialect containing the familiar sounds of the Society Islands.

After landing at Kaua'i and Niihau, Cook sailed north in the spring, eventually making it through the Bering Strait to 70° 44', where the

islands down the chain. Such was inter-island communication.

After Maui, the two ships nearly circumnavigated the Big Island, Hawai'i, before anchoring at Kealakekua Bay. The year before, in Tahiti, much to his amazement, Cook had seen an islander repeatedly surf a canoe. "I could not help concluding that this man felt the most supreme pleasure while he was driven on so fast

until the Big Island had he witnessed a man riding a wave while standing on a board. Though surfing was practiced widely in the Polynesian Pacific, only in Hawai'i were there such perfect waves and the water-savvy people to draw the sport of surfing into the heart of the culture.

Cook is welcomed at Kealakekua Bay; note the surfer in the lower left.

THE DARK YEARS

The arrival of the white man brought all sorts of wonders to the islands: metal (the islanders would trade a fat pig for a nail), guns, cannons, uniforms, venereal disease, alcohol and a new religion. The genie was out of the bottle now, and the Hawai'ian Islands embarked on a century of cultural disintegration.

The European conquistadores, explorers, adventurers, soldiers, traders and racists who toured the world in the glory years between 1450 and 1800 – extracting wealth, subjugating bodies and saving souls – wielded a two-edged sword with both edges working in their favor. One edge, disease, was invisible. The other edge was the white man's religion.

In the remote Hawai'ian archipelago, life was simple. These people had 50 words for sweet potatoes and no word for measles; they had a dozen words for sex but no word for venereal disease. Following Cook's arrival, an estimated population of 400,000 was destroyed by European viruses and bacteria until, in 1890, there were only thirty or forty thousand native Hawai'ians left alive, and most of them were deep in the throes of profound cultural aftershock. As the old order crumbled, the ancient surf culture, too, disintegrated.

Many healthy enclaves of surf culture existed when the first missionaries arrived in the early 1800s. Not only did these missionaries impose a strict Protestant paradigm on an exuberant people while diseases destroyed their bodies, but they also confined them to "modest" attire, forced them to speak in a new tongue and discouraged them from casual sex, gambling and playing in the ocean. Surfing's association with nakedness, sexuality, wagering, shameless exuberance, informality, ignorant joy and freedom were counterproductive to the designs of the church fathers, who, curiously, wound up owning most of the land in the islands.

Mark Twain, who visited the Sandwich Islands in the mid-1860s as a reporter for the *Sacramento Daily Union*, described the missionaries as, among other things, "ignorant of all white human nature and natural ways of men." He would later publish a book of his travels, *Roughing It* (1872), that would introduce surf bathing to a large number of mainlanders.

While Christianity flourished, the outward form of the Hawai'ian culture contorted, twisted, turned and disintegrated. By the mid-19th century the combination of Christian training, an increasingly organized and commercial economy, and diminishing numbers of Hawai'ian natives had reduced the sport of surfing to an occasional, almost rare, curiosity.

Were it not for a few small enclaves and isolated individual practitioners, surfing might well have disappeared during the 1800s.

THE RENAISSANCE

By the turn of the century, the islands had become a U.S. territory, the population of full-blooded Hawai'ians had been decimated, the natives were mostly Christian, and surfing had regressed by at least a hundred years. About a quarter of the surviving Hawai'ians lived in Honolulu on the island of O'ahu, where the few remaining surfers congregated at various spots along the beach at Waikiki.

Surf Hawai'ian

Aloha: Literally, "'alo" means experience and "ha" means the breath of life, commonly used today to mean hello, goodbye, love, mercy, compassion.

Haole: The coming of the foreigner (white man) and the handshake as a greeting created the word "ha 'ole," meaning without the breath of life, foreigner, white man.

He'e nalu: To surf, surf rider.

He 'ó 'la ka mea háwáwá I ka he'e nalu: The unskilled surfer tumbles [Kook!].

Kaha nalu, he'e umauma: Bodysurfing.

Kahuna: A priest, a class unto itself. A kahuna would pray for rain, abundant crops or relief from sickness or trouble and also use the powers of prayer for sorcery, sending evil spirits on errands of death, sickness, entrapping spirits and weather prophecy.

Kai emi, nalu miki: Receding wave.

Kai pi'i, nalu pu: High wave.

Kai po'i, nalu ha'i: Breaking wave.

Malu ha'i lala: Wave that breaks diagonally.

Nalu: Surf, ocean, wave.

Nalunalu: Rough wave.

Pae: To mount or catch a wave.

Pae i ka nalu: To ride a wave in to shore.

Papa-he-nalu: Surfboard.

Wahine: Woman, female surfer.

Captain James Cook and his men found it in their hearts to occasionally shoot an islander in response to some theft or threat. This eventually wore out Cook's welcome, and he was killed in a sudden and rare outburst of self-defense at Kealakekua Bay, on the Big Island of Hawai'i, on Sunday, February 14, 1779. The incident inspired artist Craig Stecyk's surreal sculpture, "Homage to Capt. Cook."

A growing number of mainland *haoles* (white people or foreigners) were coming to Waikiki as tourists or to live, and they found the Hawai'ian surfers a curiosity. When Jack London and his wife, Charmian, arrived in 1907, they were among an increasing number of people coming to the islands to enjoy the climate, culture and peaceful solitude for which Hawai'i was becoming well known. The celebrated lion of adventure literature was riding the crest of notoriety on the heels of a string of successful novels and was in great demand as a writer for magazines. When he saw a couple of Hawai'ian surfers performing their ancient art in the waves off Waikiki, he knew he had a story he could sell.

London's stirring description of the sport, published in the October 1907 edition of *A Woman's Home Companion*, included an account of his own attempts: "I tried for a solid hour, and not one wave could I persuade to boost me shoreward."

That same year, London would meet up with two men, adventurer and businessman

By the early 1900s, Hawai'i was attracting well-to-do travelers who were amazed at the wave-riding of the islanders. Despite Mark Twain's earlier admonition that, "None but natives ever master the art of surf-bathing thoroughly," Jack London (OPPOSITE, with his wife Charmian) gave it a try and published an enthusiastic account of surfing at Waikiki (shown ABOVE ca. 1910). Soon, the sport became virtually synonymous with the allure of this island paradise.

Alexander Hume Ford and local waterman George Freeth. The importance to surfing of their meeting at this particular time cannot be overstated, for it marked the beginning of surfing's 20th-century renaissance.

Stoked by London's timely appearance and passion for surfing, Ford was determined to form the world's first legitimate surfing organization, the Outrigger Canoe and Surfboard Club. A flurry of hotel construction was chewing up beach frontage, and the surfers' hangouts and board-storage areas were being eliminated one by one. For $5 per year, Ford secured a 20-year lease on an acre of beachfront and built the grass shack that was to be the first of several Outrigger clubhouses.

Three years after the creation of the Outrigger club, another group of surfers, swimmers and canoeists organized the Hui Nalu, a surf club whose members were predominantly Hawai'ians. The Outrigger was an almost strictly *haole* organization, and the two groups often went head-to-head in competition in the surf.

Formation of the Outrigger Club and the attendant publicity had a galvanizing effect on surfing and canoeing. By 1911, observers noted that the waves of Waikiki were starting to get a little crowded. When Jack and Charmian returned in 1915, the Outrigger Club had some 1,200 members, "with hundreds more on the waiting list, and with what seems like half a mile of surf-board lockers," wrote Mrs. London. Surfboard riding was becoming quite the local craze. Meanwhile, another seed had been sown...in California.

At the turn of the century, George Freeth, an Irish-Hawai'ian, was the best surfer at Waikiki (and therefore in the world). Henry E. Huntington, a Los Angeles industrialist, had heard of the 23-year-old's superb abilities and, in the summer of 1907, invited him to California to help promote the new Los Angeles–to–Redondo Beach rail service and a giant new saltwater plunge at its seaside terminus. Freeth was hired to give public demonstrations of Hawai'ian watersports, especially surfing. The event was heavily publicized, and thousands turned out at the beach to watch him ride the waves in the South Bay surf.

The coincidence of Freeth's visit to the mainland and the appearance of London's article occured at a moment in time when, assisted by new mobility (both trains and automobiles), Southern Californians were flocking to the seaside in ever-growing numbers as they gained a new appreciation of the extraordinary playground at their doorstep. Luckily for surfing, this combination created a new awareness for the sport, and the beginning of a new subculture took its first step forward.

THE BIRTH OF MODERN SURFING

With the coming of the *haole* tourists to Hawai'i, the loose-knit crew of surfers left behind by Freeth was recruited to teach newcomers about the waves and surfing. Among these fun-loving Waikiki "beach boys" was Duke Kahanamoku. Born in 1890, Duke developed into a phenomenal waterman and athlete and is remembered today as the father of modern surfing.

The epicenter of surfing's renaissance was Waikiki Beach; the Outrigger Canoe and Surfboard Club (ON THE LEFT) was founded in 1907 by Alexander Hume Ford. Waikiki beachboy George Freeth (ABOVE) introduced the sport to Southern California that same summer. However, in 1885, three young Hawai'ian princes (FAR LEFT), attending school in Northern California, surfed at the mouth of the San Lorenzo River in Santa Cruz, riding surfboards milled from local redwoods.

By the 1910s, surfing was developing a critical mass, and dozens of surfers and paddlers – sometimes more – began to crowd the waves with their antics. Olympic gold medal swimmer Duke Kahanamoku was the poster boy for the 1914 Mid-Pacific Surf Carnival, and posing with a surfboard became de rigueur proof you'd been to the isles. The population of beach boys working the sand in front of the Waikiki hotels grew along with the dramatic increase in tourists, many of them hoping to have the experience of riding a wave. The larger boards that Duke Kahanamoku (ABOVE, front row, fourth from right) introduced made it possible for surfers to ride tandem, allowing a beach boy to take a *haole* client out into the surf. That some of the visitors looking for a guided surf session were young women contributed to a lusty beachboy mystique.

The Duke at Freshwater

In December 1914, Duke Kahanamoku was invited by the New South Wales Swimming Association to come to Australia. There, after breaking his own world freestyle record for the 100 meters (53.8 seconds) at the Domain Baths in Sydney, the Olympic champion decided to show the locals how to walk on water. This was extremely new and exciting to the Australians, who had only recently won the right to bathe in the ocean during day-light hours.

On December 23, 1914, the surf was up and Duke gave his demonstration to the throngs at Freshwater (now Harbord) just north of Manly Beach near Sydney. The conspicuously dark-skinned Olympian with the jet-black hair and the huge feet surfed for almost three hours straight, showing the Aussies every trick in the book, including the ever-popular headstand ride. Duke further delighted the crowds by surfing tandem with one of the local ladies, one Isabel Letham.

So the seed was planted, and Australia was on its way to becoming a unique surf culture, one that for years kept surfing under the control of lifesaving authorities in a highly regimented interpretation of the "beach boy" concept.

Duke surfed for several hours at Freshwater, riding most waves right up onto the sand. The surfboard, which he'd shaped for the occasion, was ceremoniously delivered to the beach by wagon.

Duke wasn't just a surfer – he was one hell of a swimmer. In 1912, with his size-13 "*luau* feet" fluttering in the celebrated "Kahanamoku kick," he took the gold medal in the 100-meter freestyle at the Olympic Games in Stockholm, Sweden.

After the Olympics he was feted like royalty as he toured Europe and the United States, giving exhibitions, swimming in meets and earning the nicknames "The Human Fish," "The Bronze Duke of Waikiki" and "The Swimming Duke."

During this time Duke revealed the sport of surf riding to the crowds on the East Coast beaches of Atlantic City and Nassau County as well as Corona del Mar and other California beaches. The effect of Duke following on the heels of Freeth was electric. Clusters of new enthusiasts were inspired to take up the sport wherever Duke showed audiences how to walk on water.

With his good looks and easy grace, Duke also attracted attention in the world's emerging film capital, Hollywood. Over the following decades, in a total of seven films, he was enlisted to play a variety of minor roles, from Indian chiefs to Arabian princes, but he didn't actually play the role of a Polynesian until he was cast with John "Duke" Wayne in *Wake of the Red Witch* in 1948. Any role the man took on seemed to fit him perfectly, but Duke's greatest legacy is as ambassador for the sport of Hawai'ian kings.

Duke Kahanamoku's celebrity status put him in the company of stars (shown ABOVE with John "Duke" Wayne in *The Wake of the Red Witch*, 1948) and other famous people. He became the universal symbol of surfing and the aloha spirit.

TOP: A postcard from the era shows the many ways people had fun in the surf.

What Is Surf Culture?

Early observers with a heightened sense of adventure and an appreciation for physical aesthetics, such as Mark Twain and Jack London, found the "pastime" of surfing noble and praise-worthy. But early missionaries and visitors with Calvinist and Victorian mores found it pagan, immoral and corrupting. Ironically, these polarities continued to dominate the popular opinion of surfing until very recent times.

As in the ancient Polynesian past, there are inherent rites of passage in the development of surfers today, and those rites of passage lead to membership at various levels within the society. Surf culture has an abundant and rich history, as well as a unique system of rituals, distinctive language elements, symbolic elements, a loose tribal hierarchy, and unique lifestyle characteristics that have been broadly imitated and emulated throughout the world.

"Jeux Haviens" – a romanticized vision of a warm-water Polynesian paradise where naked nymphs surf upon the billows!

INSET: 200 years later, surfer/ innovator Tom Morey taps the source in Bali.

Tom Blake and the Hollow Board

Tom Blake was a good surfer and an *excellent* paddler. Working to come up with a faster paddleboard, Blake copied the dimensions of an ancient and largely ignored *olo* at Honolulu's Bishop Museum and began experimenting. He bored hundreds of holes into a 180-pound board with the idea of drying out the wood, then laminated the deck and bottom with plywood.

The beach boys laughed at Blake's 16-foot "hollow" creation, referring to it as a "cigar board," until he paddled away from them. Duke tried it and liked it. Then Blake took it to California, where he won the paddling race at the first annual Pacific Coast Surfing Contest at Balboa. The name "cigar" stuck, but it was no slight. In 1930, Blake patented the Hawaiian Hollow Surfboard, which became the standard paddleboard and lifesaving vehicle at beaches all across the country.

Besides being a freethinking innovator and champion waterman, Blake was a visionary surfer and a vegetarian, a pantheistic prototype for an emerging lifestyle. "Tom Blake is the obvious link between the ancient South Pacific watermen and the twentieth century Anglo watermen," says Blake biographer Gary Lynch. "Not only did he precede most other Anglo visitors to Hawai'i that surfed, he understood and adopted the Aloha frame of mind…. At the same time Albert Einstein was finishing his accepted $E = mc^2$ theory, Tom Blake was carving "Nature = God" into the sandy bluffs of what is now Malibu…. We have yet to completely catch up with Tom's final footsteps."

Tom Blake's research on ancient Hawai'ian surfboards led to the development of his hollow paddleboard. This, in turn, initiated an ongoing evolution in surfboard design that continues unabated to the present time.

ABOVE TOP: **Blake and an array of his surfboards.**

OPPOSITE: **Blake and Duke posed at the Outrigger about 1935 with one of Tom's new hollow boards.**

In 1920, Duke passed through Detroit. He and a group of fellow Hawai'ian swimmers were giving exhibitions on their way home from the Olympics in Antwerp, where Duke had once again gold-medalled the 100-meter freestyle, and they'd slipped into a theater to catch themselves on a talkie newsreel. There, a young Wisconsin lad, Tom Blake, met Duke and was so impressed by his energy and charisma that he immediately decided to devote his life to the great Hawai'ian watersports – swimming, paddling and surfing. In 1924, at age 24, Blake moved to Hawai'i to see what Duke was up to, and, incidentally, revolutionized surfing.

The past was all but absorbed into the islands' volcanic heart by the time Tom Blake stepped out onto the sands of Waikiki. The population of young beach boys working the sand in front of the hotels had grown along with a dramatic increase in tourists, many of them celebrities, looking to have the experience of riding a wave.

Competitive paddling was a major part of the early Waikiki surf scene, although the boards being used were heavy planks with little maneuverability and modest flotation. One of surfing's first original thinkers, Blake began experimenting until he eventually created the "hollow" board, a lighter version of the 100-pound Hawai'ian boards of the period.

Blake's hollow board made surfing accessible to greater numbers of people and became widely popular as a lifesaving device. Manufactured first by the Thomas N. Rogers Company of Venice, California, and later by the Los Angeles Ladder Company, this was the first

By the 1920s, surfing was a new sport, revitalized and altered to accommodate its new *haole* enthusiasts. There were competitions at Waikiki and on the mainland, and paddling races were at the heart of the contests. Here, paddlers wait for the starting gun at San Onofre in 1940. Tom Blake and Lorrin Whitey Harrison (third and fourth from right).

FOLLOWING SPREAD:
Palos Verdes Estates was another popular California surfing area of the '30s and '40s. The rolling waves were perfect for styles and surfboards of the time. This photo, of two surfers on their planks and one (CENTER) on a paddle board at Paddleboard Cove in 1935, was one of the first water shots taken by Dr. John Ball and inspired by the photography of Tom Blake.

Remote, sheltered and desolately beautiful, the beach at San Onofre played host to the quintessential California surfing scene of the 1930s and '40s. Focused around an old grass shack and waves that were reminiscent of Waikiki, the San Onofre crowd was able to evolve its own Hawai'ian-inspired surf culture.

"production" surfboard in the world. More importantly, however, it was as if Blake's advancements in surfboard design and construction had turned on a huge lightbulb. Suddenly anything was possible. Inspired by Blake's ideas, other surfers began experimenting with their equipment, and a design renaissance was soon under way.

THE COAST HAOLES

Although Blake visited Hawai'i on an annual basis, he continued to live in Southern California, where the surfing scene was growing like gangbusters. Inspired by Freeth and Duke, and Blake's revolutionary hollow boards that made surfing easier, the number of "coast *haoles*" (as they were referred to by the Hawai'ians) swelled during the feel-good 1920s, and when the Depression hit in the thirties, one of the few things kids without money could do was go to the beach.

By the late 1920s, there was a core group of surfers – men, women and kids – living a surfer's life. One of the first Southern California surf spots to spawn a culture of its own was San Onofre on the Santa Margarita Ranch at the northern edge of present-day San Diego County. Down on the sand, the surfers found a grass shack left behind by a Hollywood movie company, and that became a focal point.

By 1935, San Onofre was the most famous surf spot south of the Palos Verdes Peninsula. On a warm summer's day, the isolated beach, with its rolling waves and thatch hut, was a mainland Waikiki. The surfers who frequented it, sometimes camping there for weeks, created their own culture. They had ukuleles, grass skirts, palm-frond hats and big redwood boards, and soon a few paddleboards, too. A prewar neo-Polynesian golden era ensued, and the big dream was to travel to Hawai'i, the home of Freeth and Duke.

Stowing away to Hawai'i became a rite of passage for surfers right up until the era of $75 airfares in the early '60s. Even for those who never actually did it, the exciting tales of the bold few became part of the legend and lore of a sport and lifestyle that depended substantially on the "coconut wireless" for its news and information. Tales of determined young surfers pursuing adventure and living on the beach on less than a shoestring were romantic, but they also painted a picture of the surfer as a person who lived outside the boundaries of card-carrying society – which, to some extent, was true.

Back in the 1930s, California surfers were escaping to out-of-the-way places like San Onofre, where there were no lifeguards and little or no outside interference – just an idyll of surf and sun. It was a culture in incubation, and every time surfers like Lorrin "Whitey" Harrison, Pete Peterson (the best mainland surfer of his day and four-time Pacific Coast Surfing Champion), Sam Reid and others returned from Hawaii, they brought a little "aloha spirit" with them. A cross-pollination was in process, and even though the old guard at Waikiki was waxing a little xenophobic, guarding its spots and its ways jealously, there were big changes going on all around them.

A fine climate and good waves combined with the increasing popularity of the automobile to make surfing accessible to more and more people. Most surfers made their own surfboards (TOP LEFT), **and out in the water, two schools of thought were evident, the Blake hollow board** (ABOVE LEFT) **and the plank** (RIGHT). **World War II interrupted the momentum, but not for long.** BELOW: **Palos Verdes guys join the locals at Hermosa Beach to celebrate the end of the War, summer of '46.**

MALIBU

About the time San Onofre was beginning to attract surfers, another new spot was discovered just north of Los Angeles – a jutting wedge of sand and cobblestone facing southward toward the approaching summer swells. If San Onofre was a place that celebrated surfing's Hawai'ian roots, Malibu was destined to become center stage for the new creative edge of the sport. Eventually, and ironically, it would also prove to be a wellspring of surfing's mystique and mass-market appeal.

Up to the time Blake and Duke first surfed there, the entire Malibu coast had been the private domain of Frederick Rindge, who had worked to preserve the integrity of the old family land grant. His strong and determined widow, May Knight Rindge, fought to stop a federal highway along this idyllic stretch of points and coves, once the sacred home of the Chumash people. In 1925, despite her lawyers and armed cowboys, the battle was lost, and the state won its eminent domain lawsuit. In 1926, construction of the Roosevelt Highway (now State Highway 1) began, literally paving the way for the opening and development of the Malibu coast.

Legal access to the coast along Rancho Malibu remained limited to private use and to those with business on the land. However, a stretch of shoreline north of Malibu Point, called Malibu Colony, was sold to the Marblehead development company, and it was here that the stars met the sea. Ronald Colman tried his hand at surfing the Malibu waves, as did Jackie Coogan, Joel McCrea and a parade of other surf-stoked Hollywood celebrities over the years.

The postwar boom in wealth, mobility and leisure time brought people to the beaches in droves, many of them to surf.

OPPOSITE: **Late-'40s summertime jam session at San Onofre.**

ABOVE: **Norma Jean Baker (Marilyn Monroe) listens in on Pete Peterson and Tom Zahn in Santa Monica.**

BELOW: **From the beginning, Malibu was an "outlaw" place. It was near Hollywood too, so it is appropriate that this is where surfing's cult of celebrity began. Malibu pier, cove and point in 1950.**

The Hot Curl Surfboard

faster, more radical surfing in the very pocket, or "curl," of the wave. Increasingly modified and refined, the hot curl boards turned out to perform better as the waves got bigger. In a clear example of technology leading the way, George Downing, Froiseth, Kelly and a handful of others took to hunting big waves in out-of-the-way places (especially at Makaha on O'ahu's west side) where they could explore the possibilities of their new equipment without the "stink-eye" from conservative old-guard surfers who rode their planks straight off in front of the waves.

Hot-curl surfing was the beginning of "hot-dog" surfing, and though the older surfers didn't much like it, the tide had turned. The techniques of the hot-curl masters would continue to have a lasting effect on modern surfing style.

The reappraisal of surfboards that followed the development and patenting of Blake's paddle-board almost immediately transformed the very nature of surfing. An immense paradigm shift was occurring. Instead of reverently reproducing old Hawai'ian designs, surfers began to experiment with new kinds of surf-boards. A series of small but ultimately rev-olutionary events would eventually change the character of surfboards and, in the process, change the way surfers surfed.

One of those events occurred at Brown's surf, a spot on the opposite side of Diamond Head from Waikiki. John Kelly, Fran Heath and Wally Froiseth were surfing there one after-noon in 1934, and were having trouble with their classic wide-tailed planks. Whenever they turned to slide along the wave's wall, the tails of their boards would sideslip, a characteristic of finless boards known as "slide ass."

Frustrated, the surfers came back to the beach, put one of the boards up on sawhorses and cut off the "hips" of the board, winding up with a tail just 5 inches wide and a vee shape in the stern. The result was incredible. "I caught a wave and the tail just dug in and I went right across, and we figured something had happened," Kelly recalled. ["Hot Curl," *The Surfer's Journal,* Vol. 3, No. 2]

The new boards were called "hot curl" boards because they allowed much

The narrow-tailed hot curl boards called for a whole new style of surfing. Blackie Makaena at Canoes, 1950.

BELOW: The hot curl crew at Makaha: Russ Takaki, Rabbit Kekai, Wally Froiseth, and Roy Folk, c. 1948.

In Malibu, like at Point Conception's Hollister and Bixby ranches in later years, getting to the waves was a case of who you knew or how bold you were. Pete Peterson was one of the lucky few. His girlfriend worked at the Marblehead tile factory, about two miles south of Malibu Point. When the swell was running, Pete would drive his girlfriend to work, slip through the fence with his board and walk up the beach to surf the perfect Malibu waves alone.

The price of such incursions, however, was eternal vigilance. Two early Malibu coast pioneers, Dave Rochlen and Joe Quigg, having made their way several miles farther into the heart of the Rancho, found themselves hiding behind the rocks at Sequit Point (now Leo Carrillo State Beach), under fire from Rindge cowboys.

Over the years the Rindge estate was sold off piece by piece, in some cases to the state.

Malibu was the place to be in the summer of '51 (left to right): Don Drazen, Mike Stevens, Robin Grigg, Dave Rochlen, Peter Lawford, Tom Carpenter, Molly Dunn, and Tim Lyons. These kids had the look and attitude that became modern surfing in the second half of the 20th century.

Planing Hulls, Potato Chips & Pig Boards

During World War II, beaches became borders — fortified, monitored, and restricted. Although new materials that would alter surfing forever were being developed in the war effort, the sport entered a hiatus. With most surfers suddenly in uniform, the only people around were a few kids, some military personnel, and a handful of surfers with special circumstances.

One of them was Robert Wilson Simmons, who'd begun paddling a Tom Blake paddleboard in 1939 as therapy after a near-fatal bicycle accident crippled his left arm. A machinist and mathematician for Douglas Aircraft, Simmons got so surf-stoked, he'd quit his job when the waves were good, and return to work when the swells died down.

By the end of the war, Simmons was focusing his considerable technical skills on surfboard design. Taking an analytic approach to the complex problem of wave riding, he integrated the Navy's newly-released hydrodynamic information with post-war fiberglass technology to create an improved generation of redwood boards that were stronger, more streamlined and faster. Simmons referred to them as "hydrodynamic planing hulls," and they were a huge departure from contemporary paddleboards and planks. His plywood, foam, and fiberglass "sandwich" boards were further innovations. In September of 1954, while surfing a good-sized swell at Windansea in San Diego, Simmons slipped on a late takeoff and never surfaced; his body was found several days later.

Joe Quigg had surfed Malibu since 1939. After the war, he bought a Simmons redwood "because they were the best," but later decided to build his own boards out of balsa, which was much easier to shape. Quigg's balsas were beauties. He made an effort to select the lightest, clearest wood, glassed it with clear resin, then matched the boards with fiberglassed white pine fins. In June of 1950, he recalls, "a gang of Malibu guys went down to Windansea, and the San Onofre guys were down there, too. It was raining, so we took our boards out and slept in our cars. When the San-O guys woke up and saw our boards lying around, one of 'em called out, 'Hey! It looks like a bunch of potato chips!' And that name stuck."

In 1952, another California surfer, Dale Velzy, got a hold of a Quigg pin-tail and decided to go into business for himself. Within a few months, Velzy had rented a place above Hermosa Pier and set up shop with a guy named Hap Jacobs glassing

Three pioneers of the "chip" surfboard — Joe Quigg, Matt Kivlin, and Tom Zahn — head home from Hawaii in 1952. Just a few years before, Dave Sykes and Peter Cole were sliding the Malibu waves on Simmons concaves (OPPOSITE TOP), but with the new balsa boards a new era of performance was about to begin.

ABOVE: Simmons' surf car with his high-speed, triple-glassed, slot-railed board on top.

OPPOSITE: Dale Velzy saw surfing's potential early on and started building boards for friends in his Hermosa Beach garage. Five years later he had the first surf shop in the world.

in the back. Velzy's philosophy of surfboard design was simple: "I tried to make boards as easy to surf as I could. Instead of taking two years to learn to surf, with the chips it would take four weeks." Velzy's new "pig board" soon caught on, and he had more business than he could keep up with.

These new "chip" boards (or "potato chips" or "Malibu chips") transformed the character of surfing, becoming the vehicles for a whole new style of "hotdog" surfing (begun by the hot-curl surfers) that would define California surfing in the '50s and '60s. These boards tremendously magnified the surfable terrain and proportionally increased surfing's exposure. Suddenly surfing, which had been practiced largely in out-of-the-way places, was happening everywhere.

Malibu Point, between the Colony and the pier, was opened to the public and became the place to be when the summertime south swells started sweeping in on the Southern California coast.

The few surfers who had enjoyed the place alone would soon be joined by others, and others still. Malibu would become the scene of a new kind of cultural localism that hardly had precedent and would soon become all too much a part of the surfing experience there.

But then, along came World War II, which put an effective stop to the powerful peacetime momentum of surfing, both in Hawai'i and on the mainland.

MAKAHA AT THE CROSSROADS

After the war was over, surfers once again shuttled back and forth between Hawai'i and the mainland, but now there was a new island mystique. On December 22, 1943, Dickie Cross and Woody Brown, two Waikiki hot-curl surfers, had paddled out through the rip at Sunset Beach on O'ahu's North Shore. A big day got even bigger, and they were caught outside in a building swell. It was the biggest surf in years – 30 feet or more. Not able to make it past the 20-foot walls of whitewater, and caught in a roaring seaward rip, they headed to Waimea Bay to try to come ashore there. But Waimea was now closed out, too. It was the ultimate surfing horror story. Woody was finally washed onto the beach, but he never saw Dickie alive again.

Perhaps the best California surfer of the late '40s and early '50s, Tom Zahn's easy poised style on glassy Malibu waves belied his considerable abilities as a waterman. A lifeguard (as were many surfers in those days), he was a prodigious paddler, completing a rugged 36-mile channel crossing between Molokai and O'ahu in 1953.

It all came together at Makaha in the late '40s and early '50s, when the potato-chip Californians met the hot-curl Hawai'ians. The resulting fusion of equipment and performance style resulted in an exciting new hybrid form of surfing.

TOP RIGHT: **Makaha winter quarters with Les Williams and Buzzy Trent at the door and a woody out front.**

TOP LEFT: **Interior with surfers and boards.**

ABOVE: **The Makaha crew, c. 1950.**

The death of Dickie Cross kept surfers away from the "heavies" of the North Shore for more than a decade. Some said Woody Brown never paddled out into the big stuff after that; not true. Californian Walter Hoffman saw Woody ride the biggest wave he ever saw *anybody* ride. It was around 1950, and it was at Makaha.

Makaha, on the west side of O'ahu, somehow seemed safer than the North Shore, even though the surf could be giant there, too. A golden curve of beach and reef on the arid leeward shore, the place was almost desolate in the late '40s, and few surfers went there. Mostly it was just the hot curl guys – Wally Froiseth, George Downing, Woody and a few others, whose streamlined boards loved the big wave faces, and so did they.

Makaha was paradise – hot and dry with offshore winds day after day. The surfers camped, fished, lobstered and surfed. It was the original "country" life and the start of the California-to-Hawai'i winter surf migrations. Walter and Flippy Hoffman, Buzzy Trent, and others came for the waves. Downing and Froiseth and some of the other "town" surfers came out to surf, drink Primo beer, sing songs and talk story.

The mix of town and country, of *kama'aina* (native born) and *haole* surfers, at Makaha brought a new energy to surfing that was different from the sport as practiced at Waikiki. Makaha was a wild place that seemed to evoke the long-ago spirit of the Polynesian roots of *he'e nalu* (surfing). The ancient gathering place of O'ahu was once again becoming a center of surf culture, and in the winter of 1954 the first Makaha International Surfing Championships were held there, combining surfing, bellyboarding, paddling and tandem surfing events. (George Downing was crowned champion.) Already, Makaha was becoming a surfing destination, and on the mainland, word was spreading fast.

In 1952, Greg Noll, Jim Fisher and Mike Stang dropped out of their California school and headed to Hawai'i. Shortly thereafter, seeing a photo of big-wave surfing on the front page of a San Francisco newspaper, Fred Van Dyke, a schoolteacher in Santa Cruz, quit his job and headed for Hawai'i with his Stanford University friends Rick Grigg and Peter Cole. Many others would join the migration. It was one of the last remaining moments in surfing history when surfing was still the sport of a relative few. The surf cultures of California and Hawai'i were cross-pollinating, and it was a time of isolated bliss and shared ideas that seemed like it would last forever.

WAIMEA BAY

One of the archetypal images of surfing is a giant wave at Waimea Bay. On a summer afternoon on the North Shore's golden sand and emerald coastline, this picturesque scoop of azure cove is a placid jewel that invites a lazy swim or a dive from the big rocks on the outer edges of the small bay. But come November, December and January, it's a completely different story.

When big winter storms pinwheel across the northern Pacific toward the Aleutian Islands, they push giant waves that rise up, darken and roar over in thundering pulses. When the waves are big enough, say 20 feet or more, most spots "close out," breaking on the outer reefs far outside the usual spots, and in the 1950s and 1960s, no one seriously considered surfing out there.

But there was one spot that stayed "open" in the huge surf: the deep-water bay at Waimea. Here the waves would march in and stack up off the point, sending up a large peak

The fabulous Calhouns: Easy on the eyes, terrific in the waves.

TOP: **Robyn, Marge and Candy at Makaha in 1962. Marge, the mother, was married to Hevs McClelland, American surfing's great funnyman, who was featured in several of Bud Browne's films.**

ABOVE: **Big-wave surfer Walter Hoffman and wheels near Makaha in '49. Scion of the Hoffman Fabrics family, he began designing Hawai'ian print shirts in the early '50s.**

First day at the Bay. After years of fear and the echo of the frightening loss of Dickie Cross, Waimea was finally attempted and successfully ridden on November 7, 1957.

SPREAD: One of the "heavies" was ridden by (left to right) Greg Noll, Pat Curren, Del Cannon and Mickey Muñoz (wiping out). The first-day crew included (ABOVE) Noll, Muñoz, Bob Bermell and Mike Stang. On that day, the sub-culture of the big-wave surfers was born.

Early Surf Films and Photography

BUD BROWNE presents

SURF-HAPPY

1960 COLOR SURFING MOVIE

Fri., Sat., May 6, 7 - 8 p.m.
LAGUNA BEACH
HIGH SCHOOL AUD.

Adm. $1.25   Kids 50c   Tickets at Door

BUD BROWNE'S
7TH ANNUAL SURFING FILM

Cat on a Hot Foam Board

"The real unsung hero, the man always in the background of surfing, is Bud Browne," wrote Fred Van Dyke in *30 Years of Riding the World's Biggest Waves.* "While the heroes are carving their names in the Surfing Hall of Fame, Bud is the photographer, bedecked with camera, wetsuit and fins, who sits hour after hour at the impact zone. He goes over the falls, shooting film of the surf heroes."

Bud Browne was the first in a long line of cinematographers to translate the exciting, often terrifying, always beautiful dance of surfers and waves onto film for viewers far away. Although Dr. John Ball had made an interesting 16mm film, *Californian Surfriders*, in the mid-'40s, it was Browne's films, beginning in 1953 with *Hawaiian Surfing Movie,* that systematically fanned the fires of stoke year after year, and gave surfing its big growth spurt in the mid-1950s.

Browne, an outstanding waterman in his own right, not only provided the first widely circulated images of hot surfing action, he created the first real vehicle for fame. Surfers who were known only at their own beaches or who were merely rumored entities, like gods, could now be seen.

Taking his one-man show (he filmed, edited, publicized, took tickets, narrated and swept up) on the road, Browne paved the "four-wall" circuit, showing his movies in school auditoriums and small halls along the California coast, making stars out of surfers like Downing, Froiseth, Buzzy Trent, Jim Fisher, Peter Cole and then Phil Edwards, Mickey Muñoz and Mike Doyle, and arousing more and more surfers with the scent of Hawai'i and the big surf. Browne's films combined small-wave hotdogging and big-wave thrills with lifestyle, from on-the-road "surfari" sequences to intricate gag scenes; his formula became the model for a dozen other filmmakers who followed in the late '50s and '60s.

Surf photography experienced a similar rise. Beyond the occasional illustration or distant photograph in early books and magazines, few images of the Waikiki surf scene came out of Hawai'i. In 1935, *National Geographic* published a number of excellent shots of Waikiki surfers taken by Tom Blake from his paddleboard. The stunning results not only alerted a much wider audience to the thrill of surfing, it inspired several young people to take up

cameras, among them California surfers John "Doc" Ball and Don James.

Beyond Ball and James, most of the still photography of surfing done before 1960 was in the form of snapshots taken by amateurs or by the occasionally curious newspaper or magazine photographer.

James, who was from Santa Monica and hung out around the Del Mar Beach Club, was immediately inspired by Blake's photos. "I began shooting pictures to show our parents and teachers what was going on," he told Craig Stecyk in an interview just prior to his death in December 1996. James' body of work would, in the end, span six decades of surfing history.

Down the coast a few miles at Hermosa Beach, a young dentist, John Ball, started taking pictures at Palos Verdes from his paddleboard with a Kodak Autographic folding camera, and later a Graph-Light camera. He had to reload after every shot, sitting out there on his paddleboard. "You had to keep

an eye on what you were doing," says Ball, whose photographs of the surfers at Paddleboard Cove, San Onofre and other spots along the coast established him as the Ansel Adams of surf photography.

All of this exposure had a price, however, and over in Hawai'i it was becoming more apparent with each passing season. "Crowds came to the North Shore – or what we considered crowds – about 20 new guys in all in 1956," wrote Fred Van Dyke. "Everyone had one purpose in common, to ride and conquer his fear of the North Shore."

OPPOSITE: **Surf film pioneer Bud Browne at Makaha Beach, 1962.**

Two early masters of surf photography:

LEFT: **Dr. Don James at Makaha in 1962.**

RIGHT: **Dr. John Ball at Paddleboard Cove, near Palos Verdes, about 1938, in a photo taken by Tom Blake.**

In California, the surf club has functioned as a social and competitive medium since the 1930s. The Santa Cruz Surfing Club was one of the first. With the advent of the "Malibu-style" surfboards of the late '50s and the "foamies" of the early '60s, Australian surfers jumped on the bandwagon and created clubs, competitions and lifestyles that were very reflective of the American surf scene that was suddenly coming their way in movies and magazines.

TOP RIGHT: Aussie surf cars of the late '50s, owned by cinematographer Bob Evans and friends.

with a sloping shoulder that tapered into the water at the center of the bay, offering at least the possibility of a safe exit to a surfer who might successfully catch one.

Each winter, Greg Noll and the other North Shore surfers had been driving over from Makaha, passing Waimea Bay on their way to surf Sunset. Occasionally Noll would exhort his big-wave buddies to join him in an adventuresome foray at the bay, but they weren't going for it. "We'd looked at it for three years," Noll said in an interview. "Everybody was spooked by the place. The ancient Hawai'ian heiau [place of worship] on the hilltop, and the old house below was supposed to be haunted, and then Cross getting killed there.... No doubt about it, the place had major mystique. You had to believe with all that bullshit flying around about the place that if you went out there you'd paddle into some big hole and get swallowed up or something. Buzzy Trent was calling me the pied piper, and saying that we'd drown like rats."

But on November 7, 1957, it finally happened. "We were driving out toward Sunset," Noll recounts, "and we stopped at Waimea. It was a clean day, not huge, maybe 18 to 20 feet, and it was me and Mike Stang, and we just looked at each other and said, 'Let's hit it.' So we paddled out, and then I looked back and Pat Curren and someone else was paddling out."

Noll claims to have ridden the first wave, though accounts vary; some say it was Harry Church. Noll explains, "It was a small set, and I took off on the shoulder, dropped in, and pulled out. The sky didn't part, the Hawai'ian gods weren't pissed, I was still alive. By this

time Pat and Mike were out there, and they got the next wave, and then I looked in and there were guys rippin' their boards off the cars! The taboo was broken. Twelve guys probably surfed it that day."

Noll recalls that the local people, who feared the place and warned the surfers not to surf there, suddenly appeared. "Almost the entire town of Haleiwa emptied out! 'Cuz the crazy *haoles* were gonna commit suicide at Waimea Bay!"

The conquest of Waimea Bay electrified the surfing community. This was surfing as an extreme sport, and you didn't have to be an aficionado to appreciate it. Watching Greg Noll (the big *haole* in the black-and-white striped trunks) drop over the cornice of a 25-foot-high Waimea wall with nothing but air underneath him made you either shake with fear or want to get over there and try it.

MEANWHILE DOWN UNDER

Surfing in Australia had taken a curious evolutionary path in the days since Australians won the right to enter the sea in broad daylight in 1902 and Duke Kahanamoku gave his demonstration of the sport of Hawai'ian kings in 1914. While the surfers continued to ride plank clones of Duke's pine board, the lifesavers developed beautiful surf boats (dories), surf skis

The Sydney papers announced the arrival of the U.S. "lifesavers" for the 1956 surf carnivals at Avalon, Cronulla and other beaches. Greg Noll (right) and crew made the front page.

Originally surfboards were built on sawhorses on the beach or in garages, but by the late '50s some shapers were setting up shop; by the early '60s, they were doing big business.

ABOVE: **Two Hermosa Beach surf shops in 1964 – Greg Noll's and Hap Jacobs', who started with Dale Velzy. It was Velzy who saw the potential and got the Hermosa kids into surfing on his boards. He called them his gremlins and the term stuck, morphing into "gremmies."**

OPPOSITE: **Hobie Alter (right) with his star surfer and shaper, Phil Edwards, the first professional surfer. Hobie saw the future of foam and pioneered the development of modern surfboard construction.**

and an elaborate calendar of surf carnivals centered around competition between the surf-lifesaving clubs. Australian surfing had remained a primitive and minor component of a complex system of institutionalized bathing, calisthenic beach safety and grandiose public display.

Although actor and Malibu surfer Peter Lawford had brought a balsa chip board along on a film shoot to Australia in 1954, no one seemed to notice. But two years later, stimulated by some bureaucratic interest in surf-lifesaving, the U.S. government sponsored a mission of top American surfers to Australia, coincident with the 1956 Olympic Games in Melbourne. This time the Aussies noticed in a big way. Led by Tom Zahn, the Californians (including Bob Burnside, Bob Moore, Mike Bright and Greg Noll) gave exhibitions at surf carnivals up and down the eastern Australian coast.

"The effect on the Australian surfer was even more dramatic than the exhibition given by Duke Kahanamoku at Freshwater had been 40 years before," wrote Margan and Finney in *Surfing: A History of the Ancient Sport*. "Every Australian surfer who watched the Americans simply had to have a Malibu board. Which wasn't easy since balsa was then unobtainable in Australia, but within weeks the first plywood copies of the boards Zahn's team used were in the water, urgent inquiries were being made of the board builders in California and the first Australian board manufacturers were tooling up for business."

Greg Noll came home with films of Australia, which aroused northern surfers' interest in the land Down Under. The cross-pollination between California and Hawai'i was triangulated, and the timing was providential. Almost at that precise moment, a salesman for Reichold Plastics walked into Hobie Alter's Dana Point surf shop with a sample of a new material for which his company was seeking applications. It was called polyurethane foam, and it would catapult surfing into a huge sixties fad.

Hobie and the Foam Explosion

Hobie Alter was a California kid who grew up in Laguna Beach and found great joy in the ocean waves. Almost no one was stand-up surfing there in those days, and Hobie was content with bellyboards and skimboards, until one day he borrowed an ultralight 30-pound fiberglass balsa surfboard from Walter Hoffman. Immediately, the 15-year-old Alter had to have one, so Hoffman agreed to show him how to build his own Malibu chip.

Once Hobie had his balsa chip, the other kids on the beach just had to have one, too. So Hobie made 'em. He set up shop in his parents' front yard, charging for materials and labor (about $20

per board). He averaged 20 boards a summer through high school and junior college. Then his dad kicked him out of the yard and into Dana Point, a little town just down the road, where Hobie Surfboards opened in February 1954.

"People I knew laughed at me for setting up a surf shop," Hobie recalled. "They said that once I'd sold a surfboard to each of the 250 surfers on the coast, I'd be out of business. But the orders just kept comin'."

With the stability, mobility and financial security of the peacetime '50s, Americans were spending more time at the beach. Teenagers had gained tremendous independence, gas was cheap and air travel was affordable. There were even a few surfers on the East Coast now, and occasionally Hobie shipped a board back there.

A Reichold Plastics salesman showed up with his new foam stuff at an especially critical juncture. Surfing was growing so fast that the only limiting factor seemed to be the availability of balsa wood, which was increasingly difficult to get. Competition for South American balsa was getting intense between Hobie and Dale Velzy. So Hobie began to test the new foam, trying to develop methods of blowing a uniform, strong and clean product that could be reliably shaped with a power planer; he moved one of his glassers, Gordon "Grubby" Clark, over to the foam-blowing project, and in 1958 they set up a foam shop in nearby Laguna Canyon. Others were developing foam boards in the late '50s, but Hobie was moving faster.

A year later, Columbia Pictures released a film called *Gidget*, based on the 1956 novel by Frederick "Fritz" Kohner, who was fascinated with his daughter Kathy's real-life adventures on the beach at Malibu. The movie told a romantic tale of a free-spirited clan of rebel hedonists who lived, loved and surfed on the beach, disdaining conventional society. Though thin of story, vaguely acted (it starred James Darren, with Sandra Dee as Gidget), and hopelessly saccharine, it hit the American youth audience right where it counted. Surf culture exploded into the mainstream.

"If that movie'd come out in the balsa era," Hobie said, "no one could have supplied 'em."

Where Waves
Come From

Earth is the water planet. About 75 percent of
the surface is covered with the stuff, the polar caps
are huge crystallized masses of it, the land is pocked
and veined with it, and much much more of it is
buried underground. If you dig deep enough, this
odorless, tasteless, transparent liquid is pretty much
everywhere.

And it's no smooth sheet of glass. There's a lot
of surface area — plenty of room for cosmic energy
to pass from the atmosphere to the surface, and that
translates into the kind of wave action the sea is
famous for. The process, like surfing, is simple but
profound: Ocean waves are generated by storms and
wind. The friction of the atmosphere rubbing over the
water surface literally pushes up ripples, which are
in turn pushed into chop, which is pushed into bigger
waves, and so on. Once these waves are created,
they advance relentlessly across and through the sea
until they strike land, releasing the wind's energy as
they break on the beaches that fringe the edges of
the sea.

A perfect (but unsurfable) wave peeling over
a shallow ridge of razor-sharp reef off Haapiti
in Moorea.

INSET: Overview of Rincon Point,
"Queen of the Coast," taken by Joe Quigg in 1947.
Bob Simmons' "AV8" surf car is parked on the
roadside with his board on the roof.

THE BOOM CULTURE

"1956 – Two black Cadillac limousines pull up at the pit on a full-bore hot summer's day in the era prior to total State control. In the limos sit the directors, leading players and author of the screen scenario Gidget. They are at Malibu to 'soak up atmosphere,' scout locations and recruit surfing stand-ins and extras for the film. While the aliens stand on the beach and conspicuously attempt to keep the sand off their wing-tip shoes, several local boys gather bags of human excrement and drop them into the mouths of the limousines' air-conditioning ducts. The cars leave, containing moguls and stars, travel about 300 yards, and stop abruptly while the cast and crew fall out of the cars and gag. Sandra Dee was reportedly observed vomiting on the center lane of the Coast Highway. Tubesteak figures if they hadn't needed air conditioning, it never would have happened." Craig Stecyk, Malibu: Curse of the Chumash, *Surfer* magazine, July 1976

By 1959, the catalytic reaction seeded by surfing's pioneers was heading up the steep part of the growth curve. The beach, with the promise of freedom and excitement, lured more and more kids from farther and farther inland, and with the explosion of foam technology and the growing popularity of the wetsuit, surfing had reached critical mass.

It didn't take long for Hollywood to take the bait. The early '60s saw an explosion of Hollywood surf movies that catapulted surfing into fad status and resulted in a worldwide boom of "surf consciousness." "The movie *Gidget* was huge," wrote *Surfer* publisher Steve Pezman in 1977. "It swung surfing into mainstream prominence at a time when it was ready to accommodate new interest, thanks to foam, wetsuits and accessibility."

The emergence of a highly mobile, rock 'n' roll-fired youth culture in the late '50s dovetailed perfectly with the subculture depicted in 1959's *Gidget*. Like 1954's *The Wild One* and 1955's *Rebel Without a Cause*, *Gidget* exposed an underground society of youth that lived by their own rules. But the film was a relatively tame piece of kitsch, with the only vaguely "dangerous" energy emitted by Cliff Robertson as Kahuna and a couple of the extras, who were real Malibu surfers. Mickey Muñoz, in wig and bikini, doubled for Sandra Dee in the surf.

Yet these three films, all set in California, form a kind of evolutionary trilogy, and although the surf rebels blink in the last reel when Gidget and Moondoggie return to the establishment fold after their close brush with life's leading edge, significant cultural ground was laid, on which a young generation would soon set up camp.

Propelled by *Gidget*, foam surfboards and surf music, the surfing fad swept the USA in the early '60s.

OPPOSITE: Enthusiam and surfboards at Padre Island, Texas.

ABOVE: Real-life surf parties didn't look a whole lot like Hollywood versions. The Dana Point Mafia invaded a Greg Noll factory party in Hermosa in '65. The mob included Hobie Alter, Mickey Muñoz and Corky Carroll.

Cast into surreality by the lens of Hollywood, the Malibu beach scene of the mid-'50s was the inspiration for a film genre and for a generation of insouciant poseurs. Frederick Kohner's novel about his daughter Kathy (center) and her Malibu surfer friends (including Terry "Tubesteak" Tracey, in the white jacket, who was the inspiration for Kahuna) attracted thousands to the surf.

After *Gidget*, surfing endured almost a decade of caricature in Hollywood beach movies. There was *Gidget Goes Hawaiian* (1961), *Beach Party* (1963), *Muscle Beach Party* (1964), *Ride the Wild Surf* (1964), *Beach Ball* (1965), *Beach Blanket Bingo* (1965) and *Don't Make Waves* (1967). None captured anything remotely real about the people and the sport. But because of their success, every year there were thousands of new surfers buying boards and wetsuits.

SURFING AND VINYL

If foam and bad films kicked off the surfing fad of the '60s, the real energizer was the sudden sound of surf music. Although music had been associated with surfing for a long time, in the past it had almost always been Hawai'ian music. Many of the surfers and beach boys of California and Hawai'i played music, and some worked in bands. Malibu surfers Tommy

Between 1960 and 1967, the interplay of social forces on the Malibu coast was cartooned in a series of goofy "beach" movies. Little Stevie Wonder made his debut in *Muscle Beach Party,* but that was about all there was to recommend this typical Frankie & Annette beach fantasy. At least *Gidget*, if saccharine, was less sensational and truer to its inspiration.

FAR LEFT: Kathy Kohner and Sandra Dee compare notes on Moondoogie on the set of *Gidget.*

surfin' safari
THE BEACH BOYS
SURFIN' SAFARI ✦ 409 ✦ SURFIN' ✦ SUMMERTIME BLUES ✦ COUNTY FAIR
HEADS YOU WIN - TAILS I LOSE ✦ CUCKOO CLOCK ✦ MOON DAWG
THE SHIFT ✦ TEN LITTLE INDIANS ✦ CHUG-A-LUG ✦ LITTLE MISS AMERICA

Zahn and Pete Peterson played with Ralph Kolsiana in Ralph's Beach Boys. Specializing in soft romantic island tunes, the trio headlined at Sweeny's Tropicana in Culver City during the winter of 1953. But they never brought the house down the way Dick Dale did.

The "king of the surf guitar" and the father of surf music, Dick Dale and His Del-Tones emerged from out of the inland dust and smog of Riverside, California. Dale was so taken with the developing surfing scene – and surfing itself – that he took up the sport in the late '50s. He was never very good on a surfboard, but he could sure as hell wail on a fingerboard.

"Sometimes I'll look down at my strings," Dale once said, "and they have a black-and-blue tint to them from heating up." Dale played left-handed with his guitar upside down, thrilling audiences from Harmony Park in Garden Grove to the beautiful Rendezvous Ballroom on the Balboa peninsula. By 1961, he was already a legend in the making; Dale and his band made their soundtrack debut in the film *Beach Party.* (Little Stevie Wonder made his debut in *Muscle Beach Party.*) Soon the halls and armories were rockin' with dozens of surf bands as the surf version of the sock hop – the surfer stomp – swept the coast, then the country.

"Surfing music was the first, and only, regional subgenre of instrumental rock as well as the first time in pop history that a style of music grew out of, and around, a sport," wrote surf-band member John Blair in *The Illustrated Discography of Surf Music, 1959–1965.* "Simply stated, surf music was an attempt to express the feeling one received from riding the waves on a surfboard."

While Dale and company defined the genre and suggested the lay of the land with their instrumental music, another musician named Brian Wilson was ensconced in his soon-to-be-famous "room" in Hawthorne, California, writing the poetry of the surf into the American heartland.

The lead singer for the Beach Boys (who originally called themselves the Pendletones), Brian's brother Dennis, was the only actual surfer in the group. Along with Jan and Dean ("Little Old Lady From Pasadena" and "Surf City"), the Surfaris ("Wipe Out") and a rash of surf bands, the Beach Boys took elements of the surf sound and wove in stories of everyday life. The alienated moodiness of songs like "In My Room," the broken-hearted up-tempo pleas of "Help Me, Rhonda" and the weekend cruising bop of "Little Deuce Coupe" captured the mood of the era.

A tribute to the power of surf music was the way surf culture rode its swell farther and farther inland. In 1962 and 1963 surf bands sprang up throughout the country. In garages and high school gyms everywhere, teenagers formed bands and played local dances. The euphoric glow of postwar America carried into the early '60s and, perhaps for the last time, pop music had a naive quality that suggested life was great and everyone was having fun. Surf music expressed this perfectly. Even though there really was no Surf City where there were "two girls for every boy" as the Beach Boys sang, it didn't matter. Surf music allowed people to vicariously share in the California dream.

The Beach Boys took surfing to the American (and then international) mainstream, connecting a universal teenage angst with the specific and appealing imagery of California and the Pacific Coast beach scene. *Surfin' Safari* was the quintet's first big album. Meanwhile, from Balboa to Bondi (ABOVE), kids everywhere were doin' the surfer stomp.

Although it started with Dick Dale and the Beach Boys, there was a spirit in surf music that anyone could do it. New bands played songs about waves and surf spots while weathering the winters in Midwestern cities. The most famous among these was Minneapolis' The Trashmen, who melded two existing songs, "Papa Oom Mow Mow" and "The Bird is the Word," to form their own "Surfin' Bird." Even after they lost the copyright to the song in a legal battle, they released a full-length album titled *Surfin' Bird*, which featured a genuine cover of Dick Dale's "Miserlou."

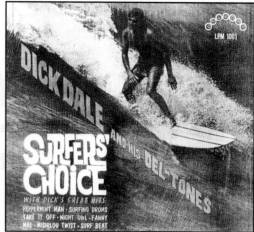

In the wake of Dick Dale and his huge local success, a slew of bands sprang up in Southern California, too. They played Fender guitars with maximum reverb and had their band's name emblazoned on the bass drum. Two of these, the Surfaris and the Chantays, achieved national success in the early sixties, both with B sides of singles. The Surfaris, a high school band from Glendora, recorded their first single, "Surfer Joe," with a B-side instrumental called "Stiletto," named after a purchase on a trip to Tijuana. The first take featured a flick of a blade as the song started. After deciding this was too punk, they decided to try a surf name and the song was quickly dubbed "Wipe Out." A nearby piece of wood was broken into the microphone, manager Dave Smallin let out a shrilly laugh and suddenly it was a surf song. DJs preferred "Wipe Out" to "Surfer Joe" and played it instead. The

Dick Dale and His Del-Tones

Dick Dale's surf sound drew on a variety of musical roots, notably rockabilly and rhythm and blues. Similar to other forms of electric rock, the surf sound was created by a heavily reverbed rhythm guitar backed by bass, drums and usually another guitar. Few chords were used; instead, monster single-note riffs were machine-gunned out through big amplifiers. According to the Fender Corporation, the archetypal surf instrumental with horn is Dick Dale's "Miserlou" (used in the film *Pulp Fiction*); with piano, the Chantays' "Pipeline"; and with a third guitar, the Astronauts' "Baja." Although "the British Invasion" of 1964 nipped the surf-music wave in the bud, Dale continued to perform throughout the following decades and was in a position to tour again with the surf music revival of the '90s.

ABOVE LEFT: **Brian Wilson's lyrics gave voice to the oceanic rhythms launched by guitar virtuoso Dick Dale.**

appeal was so great that the song was used as intro music on the British weekly pop show *Ready, Steady, Go* and soon England's scooter-riding mods had adopted surf music as their own. Even Keith Moon, the drummer for the Who, was a bleached blond playing in an English surf band when the Who recruited him in the early '60s.

The Chantays were another band formed in a Southern California high school. Their 1962 "Move It" single was backed by a song first titled "Liberty's Whip," but changed to "Pipeline" after they saw a Bruce Brown movie with scenes filmed at the famous Hawai'ian surf spot. With a surf-themed name in surf-mad 1963, "Pipeline" rose to No. 4 on the Billboard charts. Even the Ventures, a band that was playing guitar instrumentals before the term *surf music* existed (and long after), covered the song. All over Southern California bands adopted the surf sound, only to ditch it when the folk rock trend arrived in 1964. The Crossfires renamed themselves the Turtles and reached the top 10 with a cover of Bob Dylan's "It Ain't Me Babe." Not to be outdone, the Surfaris exchanged their Fenders for Rickenbackers to achieve the sound of the Byrds and released their own version of "It Ain't Me Babe."

Another wave hit in 1964. Promo stickers started appearing everywhere proclaiming THE BEATLES ARE COMING. It was a publicity stunt by Capitol Records, but it served as an ominous warning to surf bands across the land that a new style of music was arriving on American shores. Those who once looked to Dick Dale and the Beach Boys for musical inspiration now looked to the ever increasing battalions with ever increasing hair length arriving each week from England. Surf music was dead; the British Invasion began.

Although the Beatles dealt a blow to the careers of the Beach Boys and other surf musicians, the imagery conveyed by the early surf movies and the surf tunes themselves continued to inspire dreamers everywhere. In the meantime, thousands of new surfers were hooked.

MALIBU, DORA AND THE FALL FROM EDEN

In 1960, the United States was in cultural transition: Eisenhower was retiring, Kennedy and Nixon were running for president and the first American compact cars hit the market. Southern California was the fastest-growing region of the country, and the arid earthquake zone was already known for its toleration of freaky fringe people. Culture met the sand in Santa Monica, home to a thousand surf legends. The crowds at Malibu had multiplied, and a long row of surfboards leaned against the barbed-wire fence along the wall that separated the beach from the Adamson House and the last vestiges of the Rindge rancho.

A Fender guitar classic, photographer Bob Perine shot this photo (OPPOSITE) in June 1965 at Newport Beach. The surfer caught the first wave and rode in without getting a drop of water on the guitar.

TOP: Malibu surfers Tommy Zahn and Pete Peterson played with Ralph Kolsiana in Ralph's Beach Boys in the early '50s.

ABOVE: "The Little Old Lady From Pasadena" echoed the Beach Boys' marketing savvy – putting hot-rod tunes on the backs of surf tunes broadened the market. Jan and Dean skate for a publicity shot.

Surf Nazis & Bushy Bushy Blond Hairdos

The mainstream media's portrayal of surfing has always been mixed. Articles in *Time* and other magazines in the late '50s and early '60s commonly debunked the surfing mystique, associating it with the unsavory world of bikers, hotrodders and drug addicts. It got pretty twisted with the addition of the word "Nazi" to the mix, which was reinforced by the surfers, of course, always on the edge of

parody and satire, always with a kind of slapstick humor.

The Nazi stuff started with the Pacific System Homes "Swastika" surfboards of the 1930s, which were popular on the coast. In the early '60s, there were Nazi skits in surf movies, swastikas on the Malibu wall and the Windansea pumphouse, and "Sieg Heil!" stances out on the waves. Then Big Daddy Roth, described by Time magazine as "the supply sergeant for the Hell's Angels," created a line of fiberglass German-style surfer's helmets. The world's first plastic ghoul, Surf Fink, was produced, and sold in the thousands (at least) by the Revell model company. Though it sported no swastika, it was certainly grotesque. Hollywood parlayed the biker associations into the Erik von Zipper subtexts of the beach blanket movies.

The surf Nazi imagery aroused the ire of the general populace, many of whom already saw surfers as a bunch of beach bums. In the mid-'60s, *Surfer* magazine railed against the use of Nazi associations, calling them "signs of the kook" (kook being an unskilled surfer or one with an "out of it" attitude), but the term *surf Nazi* has tenaciously remained a part of the subculture's vernacular, its meaning evolving to denote a hard-core surfer who focuses on surfing at the expense of other aspects of life.

Surfer wanted the public to see a kinder gentler side of surfing – clean-cut kids wearing the uniform of Levi's, white T-shirts and huarache sandals from Mexico, or baggies (long loose Hawai'ian-print surf trunks), bare feet and peroxide-blond hair. It was just a good, clean, healthy sport. But, there was something quirky about surfin' on those waves out in California, and *Life* magazine seemed fascinated, running several articles characterizing surfers as goofy and stoked but not dangerous.

There was no denying it. Surfing was now a lifestyle that was starting to attract a curious interest from the heart of the country. It was a cult of addiction.

ABOVE: **The surf Nazi was incarnated for this editorial photo in *Surfer*. In reality, no surfer would wear such a helmet. Jim Fitzpatrick at Malibu.**

OPPOSITE: **Lance Carson's father watched Dale Velzy shape a board on the beach one day, then went home and carved a balsa blank into his son's first surfboard. By 1960, Lance was as good as any Malibu surfer had ever been. He integrated the fluid style of the purist school of surfing, à la Mickey Dora, with the complex maneuvers and nose-riding of guys like Dewey Weber. He was smooth and, in the best tradition of the best Malibu surfers, always a little surprising.**

PREVIOUS SPREAD: **Malibu's Surfrider Beach in the summer of 1962. The empty waves of the '30s and '40s now seemed a long way off.**

This was the domain of the Malibu locals who had grown up riding these waves during the war years and through the lazy '50s. They had explored the rudimentary performance tolerances of the Malibu chip boards, then created the infinite maneuvers, gestures and poses of hotdog surfing. Now they were seeing their magic kingdom overrun with inland kooks who had no understanding of surfing's historical roots, and, hence, no membership in the sophisticated peer scene at the 'Bu. The pristine days on the California coast were gone, and quality of life was taking a big nosedive in precise proportion to the rise in population. Matt Kivlin rode his last wave at Malibu on a surfboard in 1962; he said it was too crowded.

Throughout the '50s Malibu had been a place where heroes were made. The classic Malibu surf star was typically either a gung-ho aquatic gymnast in the mold of Lesley "Birdman" Williams or Dewey Weber, "the little man on wheels," or a catlike antihero like Gard Chapin or Matt Kivlin. Chasing and emulating these local heroes were the hot young kids – Mickey Muñoz, Kemp and Denny Aaberg, Bobby Patterson, the "Malibu Lizard" (Johnny Fain) and Lance Carson. Carson went on to become one of Malibu's greatest on-the-water performing artists – and perhaps the finest example of a "fusion" hero. He blended a soulful flowing style and physical subtlety with a knack for the full array of hotdog maneuvers.

Da Cat

Mickey Dora is surfing's Muhammad Ali. Here was a man with all the contradictions – a mumbler of sublime eloquence; a macho artist (he's a painter); a crude beach bum one minute, a debonair denizen of high society the next; a small-wave rider who proved himself at Waimea when there was honor (or money) at stake. His eloquent railing against the forces of growth and greed was reminiscent of other notable rebels. The only hope, he said, were the punks.

Malibu is a small-wave spot, a perfect canvas for the artist surfers of Southern California to paint their stylish poses and maneuvers. It's the classic hotdogger's wave – relatively fast but highly predict-able. A ride at Malibu could be an artistic meditation, a Zen experience far from the life-and-death tensions of surfing in the Hawai'ian Islands. Southern California writer Dale Herd eloquently described Mickey Dora riding such a wave in his 1970 opus, "Superslicksurfcat and the Ethics of the Perfect Moment," in *Surfer*: "This is Dora at his best, this time a motionless figure on a moving form, not just reacting catlike to changes in the wave but actually controlling the wave by creating the entire line of action that you watch, this the entire and profound difference between the young yet skilled surfer, the athlete only and the creative surfer, the artist."

And then there was Mickey "The Cat" Dora.

Mickey Chapin Dora (aka Miki Dora, Miklos S. Dora, MSD III): His stepfather, Gard Chapin, introduced the boy to the ways of the ocean and a life at the beach, and Dora was a worthy student – just a touch iconoclastic from the get-go. Dora's early plan to firebomb the illustrious shack at San Onofre was just one example of da Cat's outrageous scams, ruses and poses that masked a man of perception and brilliance.

A sometime stunt double in several of the early '60s Hollywood beach flicks, Dora was known to push himself even beyond the limits of his own cool. "He was hired to do stunt riding in the movie *Ride the Wild Surf*. He wasn't a big-wave surfer, but they were paying him, and he told them he could do it. The waves were really pumped up that day at Waimea. He didn't like it ... these were probably the biggest waves he had ever ridden in his life. That

day, he had made a jump from 5- or 6-foot Malibu waves to 20-foot Waimea. He was shaky, but he did it. The guy really had ability. I can't think of anyone else who could have made that sort of transition." [from *Da Bull: Life Over the Edge* by Greg Noll and Andrea Gabbard]

Taking his cues from the creative and pragmatic minds of Kivlin and Chapin, Dora saw the "new" surfing that he and a few others performed at Malibu in its peak years (say 1954–60) as fundamentally different from what had gone before. While Dora was by no means the only Malibu surfer resisting the tide of gremmies, kooks and Valley cowboys that were invading Malibu's Garden of Eden, he nonetheless became the symbol of resistance. A cult of localism, rooted as far back as the early days of Waikiki and the division of its

Epitome of the bad-boy school of surfing, Mickey Dora assumed the stance of brilliant aquatic artist driven to bitter despair by the plundering of his pristine Malibu playground by hordes of inland zombies.

OPPOSITE: Dora expatriate surfing in France in the mid-'70s.

ABOVE: Possession being nine-tenths of the law, Dora was famous for intentionally grounding kooks who dropped in on his waves.

beach into territories, became fashionable and flowered at Malibu out in the water. An area of prime beach near the pier end of the point was designated "the pit." This was where the Malibu elite hung out, and every San Fernando Valley gremmie who came to Malibu had to slip through the narrow opening in the fence and pass the pit on the way to the surf. For many, this was their first exposure to the rawest kind of profane insult and abuse – behavior

The combination of movies and magazines kept the surfing subculture in a veritable frenzy during the 1960s. Recruiting audiences for the evening surf films was relatively simple when you knew where they were.

ABOVE: **Walking the beach to promote MacGillivray-Freeman's *Free and Easy* in 1968.**

RIGHT: **John Severson at the office, typing copy for the first *Surfer* magazine, 1959.**

PREVIOUS SPREAD: **In one of his final competitive appearances, Mickey Dora withstood the commercialization of his once idyllic Malibu playground to show the casual style that had made him a generational icon.**

pioneered by Bob Simmons (a notorious verbal abuser) now became a substitute for civil conversation. The street was moving off the beach and into the waves. A new social order was in the making.

THE SURF MEDIA

Drawn into the surfing boom and in turn feeding the building crescendo was a new generation of surf filmmakers, following the blueprint pioneered and proven by Bud Browne: Shoot all winter, show all summer. Bruce Brown, John Severson, Jim Freeman and Greg MacGillivray would go on to create film classics that would inspire generations of surfers. Even Greg Noll took more than a casual stab at a filmmaking career in the late '50s and early '60s, although he was never quite sure he was cut out for this sort of thing. Noll ran the show, got the money and got everyone out of there, but he says it took 25 years off his life. "I wasn't that good on the technical aspects of those films," he admitted in a 1997 interview, "not like Severson and Bruce. I just basically loved surfing."

In 1957, backed and equipped by a flush Dale "World's Largest Manufacturer" Velzy, Bruce Brown set out to do a surf film that would promote Velzy's team riders. It was a

A Whole Lotta Surf Film in '62–'65

JOHN SEVERSON PRESENTS HIS ALL-NEW 1962 COLOR SURF MOVIE

GOING MY WAVE

TO AUSTRALIA
CALIFORNIA
HAWAII
NEW ZEALAND
PERU

FEATURING BANZAI PIPELINE, SUNSET BEACH, LONIAKEA, HALEIWA, MAKAHA, WAIMEA BAY, SANTA CRUZ, HUNTINGTON BEACH, BROOKS ST., DANA POINT, SWAMIS, WINDANSEA, TIKI'S, PENA, JR.'S, FAIRY BOWER—AUS., MANLY, AUS., NORTH CURL CURL—AUS., N. AVALON, AUS., COPACABANA, AUS., NEILSON PARK, AUS. AND MORE!

SANTA MONICA CIVIC AUD.

WEDNESDAY AUGUST 22
ADMISSION: $1.35

8:15 P.M.
DOOR PRIZE

BRUCE BROWN PRESENTS 1961's GREATEST

SURF FILM

In Person
BRUCE BROWN
Showing and narrating
his latest film...

"Barefoot Adventure"

Original
musical score
composed and
performed
by
BUD SHANK
with
Bob Cooper
Carmell Jones
Dennis Budimir
Gary Peacock
and
Shelly Manne

FULL COLOR
in
HAWAII & CALIFORNIA

. . . "Ring-A-Ding Thriller!"—Charles Champlin, TIME Magazine

The year 1962 saw a torrent of surf films. Theaters and halls in California, Hawai'i and now the East Coast were soon reeling under a barrage of rowdy, bottle-cap-flipping, fart-lighting, insult-shouting, hooting audiences of jazzed young surfers. Bud Browne's *Cavalcade of Surf*, Severson's *Going My Wave*, Walt Phillips' *Psyche Out*, Bruce Brown's *Surfing Hollow Days*, Clarence Maki's *Surfing in Hawaii* and Bob Evans' *Surfing the Southern Cross*, all came out in '62. In 1963, another Brown (Don) jumped into the fray with *Have Board, Will Travel*, North Shore O'ahu resident waterman Val Valentine showed *Northside Story in the Islands* and Grant Rohloff ponied up to the ticket booth with *North Swell*. Jim Freeman threw his hat into the ring with two films — *Let There Be Surf* and *Outside the Third Dimension*, a 3-D surf movie — in 1964, and his soon-to-be-partner, Greg MacGillivray, came out with a beauty in 1965, *A Cool Wave of Color*.

Jim Freeman
presents

HIS FULL COLOR

3-D

SURF FILM
Outside
The Third
Dimension

ONE NITE ONLY
HERMOSA
PIER AVENUE AUD.
SATURDAY
March 28
8 PM

ALL SEATS $1.75

Filmed in...
California, Hawaii & Mexico

THE SURFER

The Surfer came first and hundreds of others have followed, including *International Surfing* (now *Surfing*) and the Australian tabloid, *Tracks*. The emergence of the surfing magazines not only created a new marketplace, it synergized an audience and consolidated the subculture.

PREVIOUS SPREAD: No one was more responsible for creating popular surf culture than John Severson. Thanks to his creation, *Surfer* magazine, an industry was born and it flourished. Sevo cruising at Trestles with the Cotton estate (the future Western White House) in the trees behind him.

INSETS: Corky Carroll ad for Keds, and a fashion ad shoot featuring metal-wheeled skateboards and the Calhoun girls.

prototypical journey that would become familiar, as they surfed California, travelled to Hawai'i, drove in goofy beaters and slept on the beaches. The resulting film, *Slippery When Wet*, was narrated live by Brown and had an offbeat Bud Shank "soundtrack" (stop talking, push the button). Brown took the thing on the four-wall tour in 1958, just about the time the word *foam* was rising in surf consciousness.

While filming in Hawai'i, Brown encountered another young surfer – a cinematographer named John Severson, who was filming his first flick, *Surf Fever*, which he toured in 1960. That same year, Bob Bagley brought around a film called *Sacrifice Surf* and a guy named Bob Evans was touring Australia with a neat little travel flick called *Surf Trek to Hawaii*. The star surfer of Evans' film was a hot young Aussie kid with a Phil Edwards style – Bernard "Midget" Farrelly. It was in 1961, when Columbia came out with *Gidget Goes Hawaiian*, that Evans countered whimsically with *Midget Goes Hawaiian*, the further adventures of Mr. Farrelly, who was quickly developing skill and confidence in the much more powerful Hawai'ian surf.

The era of the single-lens reflex camera really hadn't dawned in the '50s, so when John Severson published his garage-built "first annual surf photo book" as a printed companion

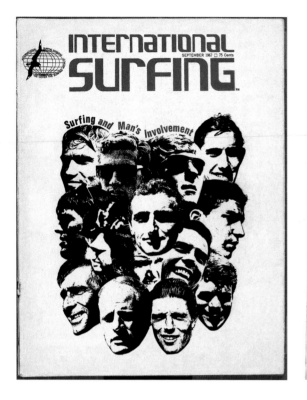

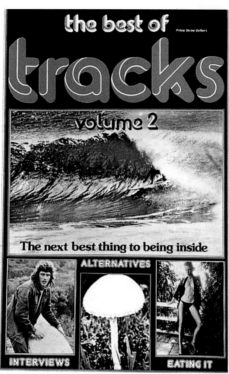

Surf Magazines Tie it All Together

The surf magazines and films of the early 1960s tremendously accelerated the development of the sport. Surfers in Australia or San Diego or Cape Hatteras could now see what surfers in Hawai'i or Malibu were doing. They could see what kind of boards they were riding, the maneuvers, the nuances, who was hot and why, and – above all – *what was possible!* Stars were created. *Surfer* soon had its annual reader poll of the best male and female surfers (Phil Edwards won the first), and *International Surfing* countered with its Surfing Hall of Fame.

piece to his film *Surf Fever*, many of the photos in its 36 horizontal pages were frame grabs from his movie. Others were shot on location by Severson or his wife, Louise. Titled *The Surfer*, the little book was a modest but exciting success – enough that Severson felt that the market was ready for a quarterly. *The Surfer Quarterly* (later *Surfer Bi-Monthly* and later still simply *Surfer*) created and defined the surf magazine and, in doing so, an industry and a good measure of the sport itself. From 1960 to 1970, *Surfer*'s per-issue pressrun went from 5,000 to about 100,000.

In 1963, *International Surfing* came on the scene as a weak companion to *Surfer*, but it struggled for identity and eventually gained some parity in the mid-1970s as *Surfing*. Since 1980, both magazines have shared the leadership role. Most other surf magazines followed the same course until Australian surfer John Witzig entered the scene. His magazine *Surf International* was one of the most artistic and innovative publications ever to come out of the field; it was joined by *Tracks* in 1970, which once again broke barriers into new territory – the brutally frank world of tabloid "surf journalism."

These and a dozen more magazines and independent films amplified grassroots surf culture. They provided another, less mainstream layer of cultural context that had a huge impact on the development of the sport. There was suddenly a market for surfing pictures, and within a relatively short period of time dozens of good photographers were out on the beaches.

Surf photography experienced a paradigm shift when Santa Barbara knee-rider and photographer George Greenough built a fiberglass/plexiglass water housing for his camera and took it under the curl of a wave to take a close-up shot of Australian Russell Hughes in 1967.

Phil Edwards: the First Professional

One of surfing's first "professional" surfers was Phil Edwards. By 1963, when Hobie introduced the first "signature model" surfboard, Phil Edwards was the guy everyone said was the best in the world, and that was worth $23 for every board he shaped for Hobie.

Edwards was the supreme California power-surfing stylist. Thousands of kids saw him in Bruce Brown's *Surfing Hollow Days* and tried to emulate that genteel but infinitely assertive drop-knee backside turn, that ankle-to-ankle parallel stance in the slick throat of a glassy tube.

Edwards immortalized himself by being the first surfer to ride a wave at the North Shore's notorious Banzai Pipeline. The photos that appeared in *Surfer* telegraphed the news around the world that the Pipeline had been "conquered." No such announcement could have been made when Waimea was first ridden five years earlier. The existence of the magazines had changed everything. They created heroes, they shared stories and they stoked the fever for surfing.

As with Waimea, the day came when the impossible beckoned – and was achieved. It was appropriate that Phil Edwards, the acknowledged "best surfer in the world" at the time, was the first to surf the Banzai Pipeline.

Advertising, which at first approached the sport generically (as in the 7Up ad), became more specific (as in the Hang-Ten ad, which featured "team" surfers Harold Iggy, Butch Van Artsdalen, Joey Cabell, Mickey Muñoz, and Donald Takayama). Eventually the iconic pro surfer was born, as epitomized in the early '70s by Larry Bertlemann (the guy posing with the Rolls). Other surf industry advertisers, like Santa Cruz-based O'Neill wetsuits, used humor and weird juxtapositions to get their point across.

ABOVE: **Team O'Neill sporting formal rubber in rural Africa, c. 1975.**

Soon, more and more photographers actually took to the water, creating a dynamic alliance between the art, capitalism and unique magic of a breaking wave. Surf stars pulled out all the stops and went for their wildest moves. They, too, wanted to be in the magazines – or the movies.

ADVERTISING CATCHES THE WAVE

It didn't take long for Madison Avenue to catch on. The surf industry was on the rise, and as the chemistry of board-making got more complicated and the volume got higher, the need for more efficient working environments became apparent. Soon surfboard factories were occupying large areas in old buildings or industrial parks. Once they were up and running, with business scaled to large volume, each company needed to maintain market share. Advertising provided the solution, at the same time creating the new job of "professional surfer."

The Jantzen sportswear company was the first mainstream business to see the viability of the surf market; they bought the back cover of *Surfer* for the first time in 1963 and remained a fixture there for several years. Ironically, their first model was Pat Curren, an almost reclusive big-wave surfer (tellingly, perhaps, he is looking out to sea, away from the camera, in the ad). Jantzen rotated a small stable of surf stars in its ads for trunks, jackets and shirts, including Ricky Grigg (who was paid $2,000 a year), Corky Carroll ($1,500 a year for the most successful contest surfer of the '60s), Jerry West (of the L.A. Lakers) and even *Surfer* publisher John Severson.

As the surf market grew, so did the industry, and by 1962 the sport had its own trade show, the Surf-O-Rama, held at the Santa Monica Civic Auditorium. Surfboard builders were experimenting with new manufacturing techniques to increase production and efficiency. Using molds, shaping machines, chopped-glass appliers and other techniques, mass-produced surfboards ("pop-outs") began to appear on the market, and though no real surfer would be caught dead with one, the belief was that novices wouldn't know the difference. But the market was more sophisticated (thanks to the magazines) than anticipated, and the pop-out companies quickly failed. So did the intrepid soul who developed and marketed a "motorized" surfboard – one of several '60s gimmicks doomed to the trash heap (or the museum of curiosities) from the moment of invention.

NORTH SHORE CRITICAL MASS

Thanks to the three M's (movies, magazines and music), surfing's critical mass was almost everywhere. Hobie was soon selling more surfboards on the East Coast than anywhere else, and young surf stars from Florida were appearing on the scene – hot kids like Claude Codgen,

Mike Tabeling and Gary Propper. Propper made so much money from royalties on his Hobie signature boards that he became the highest-paid surfer of the 1960s.

Meanwhile, where once the *haole* surfer was a relative rarity in Hawai'i, now the beaches of Makaha and the North Shore of O'ahu were dominated by surfers from the mainland, mostly Californians. At times this made for ugly interracial tensions, and the stories of fights and punchouts between *haoles* and the *mokes* (a derogatory term for local Hawai'ians) have become part of the lore of the pioneering years of big-wave surfing. Local tolerance for packs of half-naked and penniless surfers in their rusted cars, living 10 to a shack and stealing coconuts and passion fruit to survive, was ebbing.

Nevertheless, with the Pipeline and Waimea barriers broken, the North Shore taboo began to erode, and more and more surfers, bringing ever-better equipment, arrived to challenge the winter "heavies." Some surfboards were also being built on the island now. Malibu surfer Dave Rochlen came over to Honolulu and established Surf Line Hawaii with partner Fred Schwartz. The first shop in the islands to offer multiple mainland surfboard brands, along with repairs and rentals, Surf Line created an industry presence in Hawai'i. Soon several other shops opened their doors in Honolulu and elsewhere in Hawai'i, and the manufacturing of the most contemporary kind of equipment returned to where it all began.

Greg Noll (OPPOSITE, at the Pipeline) continued to push the big-wave envelope until 1969, when he took off on the largest wave ever ridden at Makaha. Even on the North Shore, however, versatility and board-handling were what won contests and recognition in the '60s.

TOP: **Jock Sutherland, a switch-foot surfer, was a master in any size; shown at the Pipeline.**

ABOVE: **East Coast stars Gary Propper and Claude Codgen enjoyed great contest success in the '60s.**

The Surfer

The surfer is a strange sort of amphibious creature, a throwback to an ancient past, a messenger from a distant and future world. A practitioner of an activity born long ago in remote Pacific islands, the surfer has always marched to a different drummer, certainly a different drummer than traditional European culture.

Surfers are tuned to the rhythm of the tides and the cycling onslaughts of storm and swell. To surf with enough regularity to be proficient (and surfing's more fun if you're good), you must be able to arrange your life to be where the surf is happening. And when it's happening, you want a piece of it, so you live with a dual awareness, an acquired extra consciousness that's constantly monitoring the situation, waiting for the call. "Hey, this is Ed. The point is perfect, let's hit it!" Surfers are always ready to turn on a dime.

To surf is to travel, and the surfer is a nomad. "The Beast" at Velzyland, c. 1962.

INSET: David Nuuihwa contemplates the paradoxes and prepares to surf at the 1972 World Contest in San Diego.

The major Hawai'ian surf spots were getting crowded by the mid-'60s. With a growing number of cinematographers and photographers on the beach (and soon in the water), the number of surfers looking for the power and the glory was also on the rise. Out in the country, visiting surfers and mainland transplants (like Fred Van Dyke, Ricky Grigg, Peter Cole, Buzzy Trent, Butch Van Artsdalen, Jose Angel and a hundred others) met and blended at a dozen major spots with ever-increasing numbers of young local surfers like Barry Kanaiaupuni, Eddie and Clyde Aikau, Tiger Espere, Jock Sutherland and Joey Cabell. As the numbers grew and the local economy began to consider surfers a resource, the buzz got out that the North Shore was "happening," spectators began to show up, young women turned out to admire the hard-bodied surfers (and some came to surf), and soon broader media interest developed.

SURFING GOES COMPETITIVE

Competition has always played a role in surf culture. In ancient Hawai'i, chickens, canoes, wives and lives were all fair game in betting when the surf was up. Revived in Waikiki early in the 20th century, surfing contests had emphasized paddling competition, sometimes over distances of 10 or 20 miles. In the past, riding waves was seen more as an expressive and less as a measurable activity, but in surf club championships in California in the 1930s, wave riding began to be seen as a central competitive discipline. Surf clubs – from the Outrigger and the Hui Nalu in '20s Waikiki, to the Palos Verdes and Long Beach surf clubs of the '30s–'50s, to the Windansea and Malibu clubs of the '60s – provided

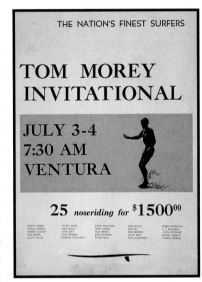

the context and incentive for competition, and most modern surf contests prior to the mid-'60s were between surf clubs.

Although vaguely antithetical to a subculture that was otherwise notoriously "hang-loose," structured competition, grounded in interclub rivalries in the U.S. and Australia, began to flourish. The better surfers of the '60s emerged out of these organizations and the competitions between them – Mike Doyle, Midget Farrelly, Ricky Irons, Nat Young, Corky Carroll, Mark Martinson, Steve Bigler, David Nuuhiwa, Mike Purpus and a hundred other name surfers earned their reputations in contests.

The first surfing contest to offer significant prize money was the Tom Morey Invitational – "25 Surfers Noseriding for $1,500" – in Ventura, California, on July 4, 1965. The rules were simple: The winner would be the one who accumulated the most time standing on the front 25 percent of the surfboard in 14 rides. Mickey Muñoz won by .7 seconds (by a judging error; Mike Hynson of San Diego actually won), and the event caused quite a stir.

The Morey contest not only stimulated noseriding as a technique, it stimulated design thinking in a way the sport hadn't seen since Velzy went off in a paroxysm of weird experimentation (Bump, Pig, 7-11, et al.) in the late '50s. Muñoz rode a Hobie board shaped by

The essence of surfing is grace under pressure. Joey Cabell epitomized the concept during the 1965 World Contest in Peru, where he entered the ring for the first time and knew exactly how to face the bull – in surfer style.
ABOVE: **Pat Curren and his son, Tom.**

Toes on the Nose

Standing on the tip of the nose of a surfboard, even putting the toes of one foot (or both feet) over the tip of the board, is one of the most difficult maneuvers in surfing, and in 1964, that single maneuver, in all of its variety, had captured the attention and affection of nearly every surfer on the planet. Noseriding was God, and the best noserider in the world was a skinny Ala Moana surfer named David Nuuhiwa.

Shock waves rippled through the California surf scene when Nuuhiwa moved to the coast in the early '60s. The kid's ability to stand on the nose, seemingly for minutes (actually 10 to 20 seconds), convinced the top surfers that they were being overtaken on the evolutionary ladder. "David arrived on the coast and immediately occupied center stage," recalls surfer Craig Stecyk. "Nuuhiwa's precociousness ushered in the era of high-performance noseriding."

Noseriding was such a clear act of ability, such a public demonstration of surfing prowess that was so easy to understand, it virtually became synonymous with surfing. "You're a surfer? Can you hang ten?" That was it: 10 toes over the nose. Hanging five was fine, but if the back foot was too far back, they called it a "cheater five."

David Nuuhiwa didn't introduce noseriding and hanging ten to the mainland — surfers had been doing it for years. But David (he was always called "David," so big was his "mysto" factor) made it an art form.

For several years prior to the 1966 World Contest in San Diego, noseriding was the most respected and admired maneuver in surfing. As a result, David Nuuhiwa (ABOVE) became the sport's most respected and admired surfer. The most successful competition surfer of the 1960s was Corky Carroll (OPPOSITE), shown testing the Hobie noserider that won the 1965 Tom Morey Invitational noseriding contest.

Phil Edwards with a beautiful concave scooped under the nose, and its success led to a flurry of noserider models, which dominated the mainland surfboard market for the next few years. Surfboard shops reaped the windfall as the demand for "new" and "different" brought a new cycle of fashion to the sport. Contest creator Morey — part mad scientist, part dream merchant, part surfer — would go on to create the Boogie Board™, the short, square-nosed, soft foam bellyboards that would one day be used by millions of people worldwide.

AUSTRALIA AND THE FIRST WORLD CHAMPIONSHIP

When the crew from *The Endless Summer* flew in from South Africa, they learned too late that the best waves in Australia come in the winter. But they arrived in time for a summer of small waves and new friends, notably a kid by the name of Robert Young. Nicknamed "The Gnat," Young was a rising star from the northern Sydney beaches who had just become the country's junior champion. He had a brash naturalness and ease, and a good presence, so Bruce Brown worked him into the film. They also encountered an old friend from Hawai'i, Midget Farrelly, who was already the most famous surfer in Australia. Cinematographer and publisher Bob Evans had been quick to pick up on Farrelly's extraordinary surfing ability, boyish innocence and agreeable disposition and made him the star surfer of several of his films and the subject of regular magazine articles. When Nat Young displaced Farrelly at the top of the competitive and cultural pyramid in the mid-'60s, a rift developed between

While the Yanks were busy riding the nose, the Australians were trying "total involvement."

ABOVE: **Midget Farrelly "quasimodo" at Long Reef in '61; winner of the '64 World Contest and runner-up in '68 and '70, Midget put Oz on the map. Bob McTavish (**TOP **at Long Reef in '67), led the paradigm shift, first to vee-bottoms, then to radically shorter boards.**

the two that never healed (they even wrote competing surfing columns in the two main Sydney newspapers). Yet at times their similarities (for instance, both emulated Phil Edwards) seemed as strong as their differences.

Farrelly and Young were not the only excellent surfers to come out of Australia in the '60s. Evans knew that the inherent coastal orientation of Australia made it a surfer's paradise and that the Aussie kids were damn good. He also was heavily invested in surfing, so he conceived and produced the first World Surfing Championship, which was held at Manly, near Sydney, in 1964. Remarkably, the contest attracted the best surfers from Hawai'i and California, as well as Peru, Great Britain and other countries. Vast crowds swarmed Manly's broad beach and bluffside, and the championship was a huge success. Not surprisingly, in less than unanimous judging, Farrelly was the popular winner and became the sport's first world champion.

Some of the best American surfers stayed after the contest to travel and surf in Australia, notably Hawai'i's Joey Cabell, whom many said should have won the Manly contest. Cabell surfed with a poised style and a penchant for speed that earned him his nickname, "The Gazelle." Cabell's surfari up the coast to Angourie and other spots opened his eyes to the quality of Aussie surf, and his surfing opened the eyes of the Australians to what was possible on their own waves. In the wake of Evans' event, the popularity and quality of surfing in Australia took a huge leap forward.

Worlds collided at the 1966 World Surfing Championship in San Diego. Wins by Farrelly in Australia in '64 and Peruvian star Felipe Pomar in Peru in '65 (the first "official" world contest) seemed to indicate it was California's turn. It was fully expected that David Nuuhiwa and his 10-second noserides would carry the day. But Nat Young came to California, the hotbed of the surf culture, and proceeded to demolish the opposition with a demonstration of powerful no-frills surfing that embarrassed the Californians and shocked them out of their hang-ten reveries.

Young's victory over Nuuhiwa, Corky Carroll, Jock Sutherland, Mike Hynson and all the rest of the long-stick tip-riding surf stars ushered in a period of confusion, nationalism and defensiveness as the California "hot performers" tried to minimize what had happened at the hands of the Aussie "total involvement" philosophy, which rejected California-style surfing's exaggerated poses and gimmicky surfboard designs. The Aussies had a new George Greenough/Bob McTavish-inspired vision of what surfing was, and it was revolutionary in its simplicity: set your mind free!

PLASTIC MACHINES: THE SHORTBOARD REVOLUTION

While the Yanks worked on damage control, Nat returned to Australia, where he found that things had changed. Suddenly his own 9'4" board (which he'd left back in California to be admired), was as obsolete as the noseriders it had vanquished. Short was the operative word

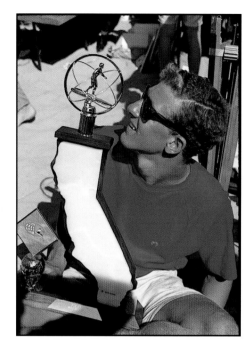

ABOVE: **Nat Young with the '66 trophy.**

BELOW: **Nat at Honolua Bay where it all came together in '67.**

Nat Young and the Involvement School

"I first met Nat in Sydney," recalls Bob McTavish. "He was living at Collaroy, and I was shaping at Scott Dillon's factory in '62. Nat was just a raw kid – gangly, but with incredible talent. He was mimicking Midget for the first couple of years, and Midget was mimicking Phil Edwards, but I had no doubt that someday Nat would rise over that and become his own man, and then he'd be incredible."

At a chance encounter with Nat in the parking lot at Narrabeen one day, McTavish laid out the facts of life. "If there are two trains on the same track," he said, "one can never overtake the other. But if you change tracks, you can roar off at your own speed." Nat took the counsel seriously, breaking away, shedding Edwards, Farrelly and even McTavish in one fell shift of attitude. He simply became himself. "With his move into the involvement school of thinking in '65–'66, Nat became liberated... and that was on long boards!" says McTavish.

now. "When [Nat] came back, he spent a period of fame as the world champion, being feted around the city," recalls Bob McTavish. But when he came north again, "he got a shock to see that we'd suddenly discovered shortboards, and he rapidly tried to catch up, and he did. He caught up and overtook all the Australians. By late '67 he was looking pretty amazing."

Nat Young dropped out of sight and into the creative kitchen that was brewing new ideas up the coast in Byron Bay. What emerged were short wide-tailed boards with vee-shaped bottoms and deep flexible Greenough-style fins. The boards were 8'6" and getting shorter. John Witzig looked at McTavish's latest and exclaimed, "It looks like a plastic machine!" and the name stuck. A hot new kid from Victoria – goofy-foot Wayne Lynch – single-handedly redefined the lines that could be drawn on the face of a wave. It was a very exciting and explosive time, and it really seemed like anything was possible.

It was at this time that California's Windansea Surf Club paid a visit to Australia to compete in a post–World Championship showdown. Along for the ride to document the event was a young man named Eric Blum, an associate producer with 20th Century Fox who hoped to make "a truly professional film on the sport." The movie was entitled *The Fantastic Plastic Machine*, and it virtually ignored the Windansea boys to feature Young, McTavish and Greenough. "Nat was the first surfer I had ever met whose ideas matched his incredible surfing skills," gushed an enthusiastic Blum. While the film never received wide distribution, *The Fantastic Plastic Machine* clearly illustrated the shortboard paradigm shift: It wasn't simply a change in equipment that was sweeping through surfing, it was a change of consciousness.

In the late '60s, Nat Young, Wayne Lynch and another red-hot Aussie named Ted Spencer were on a filmmaking trek to some of the world's best surf spots with John Witzig and his brother, Paul. They encountered perfect waves at Honolua Bay. The resulting photos of Nat and McTavish showing a new style of surfing appeared in *Surfer* and seemed to kick the shortboard revolution into a whole new gear. Witzig's film, *The Hot Generation*, soon followed, and the closing sequences of the Aussies surfing their vee-bottoms at Honolua Bay created an incredible sensation when the film toured American and Australian halls and auditoriums on the four-wall circuit.

What the surfboard industry initially resisted (trying hard not to have to eat its inventory of longboards) now began to pay off as it became clear that virtually every surfer in the world was suddenly in the market for a new "stick"; one by one, all of the manufacturers got behind the shortboard program. But the industry had changed; a great democratization had occurred, and it would never be the same as it had been in the early '60s, when just a dozen or so manufacturers controlled the sport.

Two of the four prime movers in the shortboard revolution: George Greenough (ABOVE), the California theorist and inspiration, and Bob McTavish (TOP), the architect and primary test pilot of the vee-shaped bottom and early shortboards. Nat Young and Victoria's goofy-foot Wayne Lynch were the other two.

The Endless Summer

In 1963, filmmaker Bruce Brown was in Hawai'i working on a new film.

Brown had begun surfing about 1950 in the Huntington Pier–Seal Beach area. After high school, he signed up for the draft and went to submarine school in Connecticut: "I'd read an article in *Reader's Digest* that if you went to sub school and got in the top 10 percent of your class, you could choose your coast, and the top guy could

happen. They'd meet someone, there'd be something to do. It was cinema verité, and everything seemed just perfect, especially the wave they came upon at Cape St. Francis in South Africa. In that sequence, Brown found his magic. When the film was finished, he knew he had something good in the can.

Brown had a new man working with him by the time the film hit the four-wall circuit in 1964. Paul Allen, a surfer, had come into the office one day

The Endless Summer

On any day of the year it's summer somewhere in the world. Bruce Brown's latest color film highlights the adventures of two young American surfers, Robert August and Mike Hynson who follow this everlasting summer a-round the world. Their unique expedition takes them to Senegal, Ghana, Nigeria, South Africa, Australia, New Zealand, Tahiti, Hawaii and California. Share their experiences as they search the world for that perfect wave which may be forming just over the next Horizon. **BRUCE BROWN FILMS**

choose his submarine." Brown finished at the top of his class, chose Pearl Harbor and then picked duty that kept him on the island, so he could surf.

The Endless Summer was a simple tale that would appeal to anyone: two surfers, Mike Hynson and Robert August, hitting the road, following the summer and the surf around the world. Brown and crew filmed in Senegal, Ghana, Nigeria, South Africa, Australia, New Zealand, Tahiti, Hawai'i and California. Things didn't always go the way they planned, but then Bruce Brown wasn't the kind of person to do all that much planning anyway. He was more in the "school of flow." Somehow, even when they had no luck with the surf, something would

and said he wanted to help Bruce promote his films. "He said, 'Don't pay me. If I make you money, I'll get something,'" Brown recalls. "It's a little hard to turn that kind of a deal down. And he was real good at it."

With Allen arranging the shows and coordinating publicity, *The Endless Summer* was a big success on the circuit — so big that Brown and Allen decided to look for a national distributor. With Bruce's easy homespun narration woven into a nice soundtrack by the Sandals, they went to work trying to sell it but came up dry. They figured a successful run in the U.S. heartland could be convincing, so they booked a theater in Wichita, Kansas, and

another in New York City. After breaking records in both theaters, they finally attracted some attention and a distributor that would let the film run as is. The reviews were great and the rest is history.

When the film finally went into wide distribution in 1966, the reaction of Kansans, New Yorkers (including the critics) and audiences around the country was similar to the reaction of the people crowding the beaches in Senegal and Ghana when Robert and Mike had paddled out and started riding waves right in front of their villages — they were stoked! Brown, too, was stoked — his $50,000 investment brought him millions.

What was the film's special attraction? "I don't know," Brown admits. "I've run into so many people who saw *The Endless Summer*, particularly back east, and said it had some effect on them. But a lot of 'em, they didn't surf, and they never did surf. It's always been a mystery to me."

Into Africa: Robert August, Terrence, Mike Hynson, Jack Wilson Bruce, and Max Wetland on the scent near Cape St. Francis. *The Endless Summer* poster was designed by former *Surfer* magazine art director John Van Hammersveld.

Aloha to the Duke

In 1967, Duke Kahanamoku – Olympic champion, longtime sheriff of Honolulu and embodiment of the Aloha spirit – died: "The great heart that had carried him to Olympic triumphs and the pinnacle of the surfing world stopped beating after a fall at the Waikiki Yacht Club," wrote John Severson. At age 74, recalls Severson, the Duke had said he'd never stop surfing: "I'll just pick up the right kind of wave and keep on riding." The man who had reintroduced the logic of the longboard went out with the emergence of the shortboard.

ABOVE: **Duke Kahanamoku brought Waikiki water to San Diego for the '66 World Contest; here he consecrates the event with a mixing of the waters. The shortboard came in when the Duke went out; he died in '67.**

RIGHT: **Nat Young in 1967 during the filming of *The Fantastic Plastic Machine*.**

Dick Brewer and the Pocket Rocket

At about the time George Greenough and Bob McTavish were experimenting with new design ideas in Australia, Dick Brewer was making headway with a new type of surfboard on Maui. Brewer was the prototype "underground" surfboard builder, a guru, literally, to a small group of the best young surfers. A former Southern California aeronautical engineer, his occupation crossed over into his predilection in the early '60s, and he wound up shaping surfboards for Bing Surfboards in the South Bay, earning notoriety as the craftsman behind David Nuuhiwa's boards. Brewer was one of the migratory flock of Californians that eventually didn't go back, and he'd been integrating the disciplines of shaping, yoga and mind-altering drugs into a new vision of surfing that paralleled what had been happening in Byron Bay, Australia.

However Brewer was working in a very different wave environment. His 1967 "mini-gun" surfboard was essentially the opposite of the Greenough-inspired McTavish designs, but also short, light and radically new. Brewer's boards were teardrop-shaped, with the wide point forward, tapering back to narrow pintails. These "pocket rockets" were specialized tools for riding Hawaii's fast, hollow and powerful waves.

Aeronautical-engineer-turned-shaping-guru Dick Brewer gathered an elite corps of surfers around him, built them small "mini-gun" surfboards to ride, and reinterpreted the shortboard revolution by adapting it to the powerful Hawai'ian surf conditions. An advocate of mind-expanding drugs and Zen awareness, he was also widely respected for the exquisite big-wave guns he built over the years.

"The so-called underground guru surfboard builders are, in reality, the workers from the major surfboard firms going into business for themselves," stated Dick Brewer in an interview in the winter of '70–'71. "There are now a thousand surfboard shops where there used to be a hundred. The surfboard industry is in better shape than ever before; it's just that all the business is no longer in the hands of a few."

INTO THE MYSTIC

In 1968, surfing experienced the greatest cultural and conceptual shift in its history as virtually the entire sport threw away its 9- and 10-foot boards and took up shortboards. In a single year, the sport was almost completely transformed. Surfboards went from 9'6" to 8'6" to 7' and below, and anyone on a longboard was surfing a dinosaur. The healthy, clean-cut, established look that had been carefully nurtured by a surfboard manufacturing industry interested in attracting new buyers collapsed in an explosion of long hair, beads and funny-smelling smoke. Psychedelic imagery flooded into magazine ads, and surfing's latent pantheistic origins bubbled to the surface in ad copy like, "There's a divinity that shares our ends, rough-hew them tho' we may…" [Rick Surfboards], "Karma: One's way of life is spirited from within…" [Bing Surfboards] and "From the Green House to the Green Room: Jacobs Surfboards are inspired by the green glory of the natural world."

The veil was thin, the shell had cracked and surfers could talk to each other with a new openness, even in ad copy. "I have aligned myself with Weber to give direction to my thoughts and experience," wrote Nat Young in a 1968 ad for Dewey Weber Surfboards.

George Greenough and the Shortboard Revolution

In the aftermath of the 1966 World Championship, another California visitor began to have an impact on Australian surfing. George Greenough was a surfer of a different sort. He surfed on his belly or his knees, riding a canvas air mattress or a short, scooped-out, six-pound Fiberglas kneeboard (nicknamed Velo) with flexible tails and a deep foiled fin, which he'd modeled from bluefin tuna's. Already a living legend among California surfers and known for speeding his gutted Highway Patrol black-and-white to obscure surf spots in search of uncrowded waves, George was a quasi-loner who was surprisingly loquacious when prompted to discuss his ideas, experiences and technical theories. Greenough was a primary inspiration for the shortboard revolution of 1966–1967.

Greenough divided his year between the hemispheres, enjoying endless cold winter power and uncrowded conditions. Bob McTavish was most impressed by Greenough's fins and began to adapt some of his "neutral-handling" high-performance ideas to regular surfboards. When the new Australian champion, Nat Young, visited McTavish while preparing for the 1966 World Championship, he met Greenough.

Inspired by what he saw, Young returned to the Gordon Woods factory in Sydney and translated Greenough's design concepts into "Sam", the unusually thin 9'4" surfboard (with a Greenough fin) on which he won the world title in 1966. Young's victory would send a shock wave through surfing and completely alter its course. During 1967, McTavish and his Aussie test pilots whacked another foot off their boards and introduced a radical vee-bottom design that ignited a world wide shortboard revolution.

TOP: **California kneeboarder George Greenough built dished-out "spoon" knee-boards with bluefin tuna-style fins and flexible tails that caught the attention of the key Australian surfers and put them on a new course. As a result, Bill Barnfield** (ABOVE) **found himself mowing foam, building boards for the North Shore crew.**

"Some people have done it with music, like Mike Bloomfield, John Mayall, Eric Clapton. What they give you through their music is basic honesty. I can only give you this through surfing and my communication with you."

The door was flung open and new winds were blowing through. Out on the water there was talk and conversation. Surfers encouraged each other, hooted for the other guy's good ride, talked board design and new possibilities. The virtual monopoly of a handful of surfboard manufacturers had been supplanted by a grassroots network of underground shapers working one on one with their customers, building boards in garages and small shaping rooms. The time for mass production and pop-outs was over, and any manufacturer who wanted to stay in business needed to sign up radical and creative team riders to hold market share. The era of signature models morphed into the era of intimate soul-brother vibrational alignment. You rode what felt good, what let you express yourself. Flower power came to the beach.

In the late '60s and early '70s, a fusillade of imaginative, idealistic and sometimes well-made surfing films, most propelled by the psychedelic soundtracks of the time, barraged surfing audiences with stoked paeans to organic bliss and tubular escape. Paul Witzig's *Evolution*, featuring the mind-altering surfing of the period's most imaginative surfer, Wayne Lynch, was probably the best example, but Hal Jepson's *The Cosmic Children*, Greenough's *The Innermost Limits of Pure Fun*, Severson's *Pacific Vibrations*, Fred Windisch's *The Natural Art*, Mastalka-French's *Seadreams*, MacGillivray-Freeman's *Waves of Change* and *Five Summer Stories*, Alby Falzon's *Morning of the Earth* and Witzig's *Sea of Joy* were each revolutionary classics in their own way. Harmony with nature, surfing as art and surfing as a tribal brotherhood were strong currents running through each of these films. As in the culture at large, there was great optimism afoot in surfing. Things had changed with the shortboard, the music and the energy, and surfing would never be the same again.

SURFING GOES UNDERGROUND

The revolution was diverted almost as soon as it began. Surfing's radical fringe found itself increasingly isolated in the postpsychedelic '70s as parties with vested interests in the sport regrouped, retooled and restyled to capitalize on an activity that fed the most exciting and charismatic subculture on the planet. The surf culture looked like potential big business and the capitalists began to move in. As Phil Dexter, visionary president of Big Surf, Inc., which built the first artificial wave machine in Tempe, Arizona, would say, "Who needs an ocean?"

At the 1967 Malibu Invitational Surf Classic, competing for the last time, Mickey Dora took off on a wave and trimmed beautifully across its dark blue-green face until, passing in front of the judges, he bent over, dropped his black shorts and exposed his naked ass to the gathered dignitaries and spectators. Dora loathed contests and the "fascist" control they exercised over the surfers, the beaches and the waves. He called contest judges "senile surf freaks."

At the World Championships in Puerto Rico in 1968, the panel of judges ignored the new aesthetic of free and radical expression and delivered a verdict based on classic old-school criteria: Hawaii's Fred Hemmings Jr. rode waves in the most critical position for the longest distances and edged Midget Farrelly to win the title. The failure of the new school of surfing to win recognition in Puerto Rico dovetailed with a growing apathy toward competition within the surfing world itself.

In Hawai'i, interest in international competitions held in small waves was minimal. "This is between the Australians and the Californians" seemed to be the attitude surrounding the 1970 World Championship on the southern edge of Australia. The best Hawai'ian surfers were caught up in a reverie of surfboard development, lifestyle experimentations and big-wave acid tests, and some didn't feel like making the 6,000-mile trip to the small town of Bell's Beach.

Of course, not everyone stayed away from the 1970 World titles. The arrival of a couple hundred hot surfers in Torquay in May 1970 kicked off a bizarre two weeks of cultural crisis. There were raids and drug busts, politics and walk-outs, crises and confusion, bad behavior and, to make matters worse, almost no surf. Forget that Corky Carroll verbally abused the wife of the local innkeeper, that all but one of the U.S. "continental" team refused to march in the opening parade, that David Nuuhiwa flew back to California in a huff after being eliminated in an early round (and while he was in flight, officials decided everyone would get a second chance) and that everyone said the whole thing was a joke. Something magical happened anyway.

SURF BOARDS by Dewey Weber

With the shortboard revolution came a new atmosphere of free experimentation. Backyard shapers were building boards in garages in California, Hawai'i, the East Coast and Australia, and the big surfboard companies lost their grip on the industry. However, some manufacturers, like Dewey Weber (LEFT), made successful transitions, often by hiring credible surfers for their teams. In Dewey's case, it was Nat Young and a guy named Mike Tabeling from Florida.

Meditation brought us flowers on cotton corduroy on Corky Carroll.

Jantzen

Rick Griffin

The shortboard revolution was coincident with an enormous cultural sea change. Rick Griffin, the California artist who began his career by illustrating Greg Noll's *Surfer's Annual*, then moved to Severson's *Surfer*, where he developed the lovable little surf gremmie he called Murphy, was soon producing spectacular psychedelic posters for the Grateful Dead, Jefferson Airplane and Big Brother and the Holding Company. By the late '60s, Murphy was surfing through time and other dimensions wearing the transcendent helmet of an ancient Hopi demigod and speaking in tongues. "Rick really gave surfers a good image for a lot of people who really didn't think

much of surfing," says Severson. Griffin's work (as well as Severson's and several other surf-artists') was featured in a mid-'60s "sport and art" show put on by *Sports Illustrated*. Rick went down on his Harley Heritage Softail in 1991. "Rick, like the rest of us, was on a mission to turn on the world," said Jerry Garcia, not long before his own death in 1995.

The '60s revolution was so powerful in surfing, it even swept up pro surfer Corky Carroll — at least long enough to don flowers and other accoutrements for Jantzen (OPPOSITE).

ABOVE: Rick Griffin at Rights and Lefts on the Hollister Ranch near Point Conception.

On the North Shore, Hawai'ian sugar fortune heir and stepson of Clark Gable, Bunker Spreckels (aka "The Player"), translated the revolution into personal terms. Dancing at the edge of the impossible, this 20-year-old kid rode tiny, thick, weird boards deep in the bowels of the heaviest barrels, amazing local veterans and traveling surf stars with his sheer daring and utter lack of fear. This "genetic space child" (in the words of Mickey Dora, who knew him ever since Spreckels was a Malibu gremmie) was dead by 1977 of an experimental life that never operated below the red line.

At the eleventh hour, faced with a flat ocean and no champion, International Surfing Federation (ISF) president Eduardo Arena reluctantly agreed to move the semifinals and finals two hours' east, to a remote "secret spot" with an excellent exposure to waves coming from the Tasman Sea. There, near a farming community called Johanna, the world's best surfers gathered in a bucolic seaside setting to compete. On hand were only the few remaining competitors, the odd friend or companion, a few members of the surf media, a couple of ISF officials, five judges, a half-dozen farm families and several grazing Jersey cows. In fading afternoon light on clean six-foot surf, California's Rolf Aurness proved his point (that short boards had gone too far) and left everyone else pondering. "Nothing can detract from Rolf's win," wrote John Witzig. "He was far and away the most consistent and aggressive and exciting surfer throughout the length of the contest."

Accepting his trophy at a simple ceremony at the Lorne Hotel, Rolf said (simply), "This is outtasight!" And then he left. It was like the day the music died. He walked off with his trophy, and he never competed again; he became a reclusive musician, and the championship – it was like it didn't mean a thing. Rejecting the gaudy metal and ego trips of competition, Wayne Lynch, Nat Young, Ted Spencer and other Aussies moved off into country seclusion. In Hawai'i and California it was much the same thing.

Surfboards went psychedelic and the industry went to strange places in the late '60s. Dale Velzy (BELOW, LEFT) adapted by shaping for other companies as new manufacturers entered the market and design theories reflected the "whatever works for you" philosophy of the times.

The shortboard revolution ushered in a new era of experimentation.

OPPOSITE: Nat Young, the consummate surfer, completely in sync at Haleiwa in December '68.

ABOVE: Owl Chapman casually slotted on the world's fastest wave, Maalaea on Maui in 1976 – "I've got a lot of alcohol in me here," he said.

LEFT: Famous power surfer Barry Kanaiaupuni loose in the juice at Honolua Bay, Maui, January '72.

White House Breaks

In California, young Rolf Aurness (son of television's James "Gunsmoke" Aurness) was on a tear, dominating the 1969 AAAA circuit with a loose unconcerned ease that baffled his more hard-minded foes. At the time, Rolf and his friend Corky Carroll were the only two surfers with professional dispensation to surf at Cottons Point (where Aurness lived). The old Cotton estate had become the Western White House, and when Richard Milhous Nixon (the dude from Yorba Linda) was in town, the beach in front of his palatial abode was off-limits. Whether or not the Hobie surfboard the lads presented to the president was a factor in their exemption, no one was saying.

On one occasion, when less notable surfers were enjoying perfect eight-foot waves down the beach at Trestles (which was off-limits anyway, but with Nixon in town it was doubly off-limits), an 85-foot Coast Guard craft was used to nudge the waveriders toward shore and into the waiting arms of the MPs. The concerns of surfers, however, were well beneath the sloping nose of the

free-world leader and his beach-roaming security staff. Fortunately for Nixon, the man next door with the large apparatus was not preparing to volley bazooka rounds onto the presidential grounds. It was merely a 1000mm Century lens, and the neighbor was merely a friendly *paparazzo*

dealing photos to *Life* magazine, in which he himself had been featured a couple of times in the '60s. That neighbor was John Severson.

Surfing at Trestles meant arrest and confiscation – if you were caught.

On the release of his decade-closing *Pacific Vibrations*, John Severson described his goals in the film: "An example of man in harmony with nature. A film to remind you of your roots. A life that doesn't emphasize materialism. Have a good time. The natural way. A witness to the truth."

It was almost as if surfing, like the counterculture, was going underground. Surf music was dead, and the music of the late '60s was Led Zeppelin, John Mayall and Jimi Hendrix. Surfers like Mike Hynson, David Nuuhiwa, Leslie Potts and Chris Green, who reputedly felt a common bond with the brothers in the "Brotherhood," were friends and inspirations to Hendrix, who assembled a word-of-mouth concert and "be-in" on the slopes of Maui's Haleakala crater in 1970 in a last-ditch attempt to cross the "Rainbow Bridge" before the unique window of the psychedelic '60s closed. A week later Hendrix was dead, and the film *Rainbow Bridge* was all that remained.

Meanwhile, the surf "industry" appeared to be collapsing; clubs and organizations were losing membership or dissolving as the sport dispersed into enclaves of localism amid rumors of environmental disaster and the background roar of Vietnam. There was a medieval taste in the air; the past was dying, the future was incubating.

The finals of the 1970 World Contest were held at a remote beach in Victoria, Australia, on the Tasman Sea. Won by Californian Rolf Aurness, the event seemed to showcase the intimate and personal nature of surfing rather than its popular face.

OPPOSITE: The way to Johanna.

LEFT: The contest was staged from Walli Brown's pasture.

ABOVE: Aurness at Malibu, summer of '69.

The Surf Spot

Where the happy coincidence of variables creates surf of excellent quality in an accessible and safe environment, that place is a surf spot. Scattered around the world are thousands of surf spots, and they vary enormously. There are the famous classic point breaks, like California's Malibu, South Africa's Jeffreys Bay and Australia's Byron Bay. There are the notoriously powerful big-wave breaks — Hawai'i's Waimea Bay, California's Mavericks at Half Moon Bay, Baja Mexico's Todos Santos Island and northern Spain's Mundaka. And then there are the elegant but hard-breaking reef breaks, like Grajagan in Java, Uluwatu in Bali and the prototypical Banzai Pipeline on O'ahu's celebrated North Shore — waves so refined and perfectly formed that their peeling progress is like poetry to watch.

The right tide, the right swell, the right help from a breeze from just the right direction, and a surf spot can be transformed into brief perfection — for a day or an hour or perhaps just a single wave. A listing of all the world's surf spots would probably be as lengthy as a mid-sized town's residential telephone directory. And similarly, a lot of names would be unlisted. Surfers call those "secret spots."

One of the most perfect wave spots in the world is Honolua Bay on the northwestern tip of Maui. Here, waves fan in from a North Pacific storm to peel smoothly along the reef.

INSET: Paddlers watch a porpoise drop in.

FROM SOUL TO PRO

"It would seem that the sport of surfing is growing towards a greater level of recognition by people not so much connected with the surfing world per se, but that of the business world, where advertising is one of the key factors for success. Frankly, I wouldn't mind taking home 7,000 bucks for finishing eighth place in a commercially organized, sponsored surfing tournament. It's a hell of a lot better than digging ditches or driving a honey wagon." Bill Hamilton, *Surfer* magazine, 1971

The apparently innocuous introduction of the shot-cord (aka the "kook cord" or the "leash") in 1971 had a huge impact on surfing. At first rejected out of hand by the "soul surfers," purists who wanted surfing to remain as pristine and uncluttered as possible, the prospect of not losing your surfboard in a wipeout (and having to swim after it) ultimately had an irresistible appeal. After the cord's first appearance in Santa Cruz, the idea spread – slowly. It simply wasn't cool to have this leash hanging off of your board, not to mention that your board could snap back and knock your teeth out. Real men didn't use leashes.

But the board didn't snap back too often, and when a leashed surfer wiped out, his board didn't tumble through crowds of paddling surfers like a loose saber. The leash actually made things safer and, though it was banned mid-contest at the Malibu AAAA in the summer of '71, it was eventually accepted by surfers everywhere.

Once a comfort zone was reached with the leash, the developmental curve of performance soared. It flung open the doors to experimentation. You could try a wildly spectacular move knowing that if you blew it you wouldn't have to swim. This, coupled with the rising popularity of the wetsuit, allowed surfers to work on improving their surfing technique. Suddenly everyone was "going for it." The tube ride (a low-percentage maneuver) became the core performance focus of the 1970s and beyond, largely because of the leash. Paddling and swimming skills were becoming a thing of the past. Technology was domesticating the sport of ancient Hawai'ian kings.

THE WORLDWIDE SEARCH FOR PERFECTION

Surfers are nomads. To surf is to seek, and to seek is to roam. To find a good wave may require traveling a good distance. To find a great uncrowded wave might take you to the ends of the earth. Bruce Brown's *The Endless Summer* was enough to show you that. Some surfers never find it; many do just once or twice in their lives. Others find it at their local surf spot. But for the surfers who really go after it, the stories are legend.

The leash wedded surfer and surfboard together and changed the face of surfing. Suddenly, you could attempt the most radical maneuvers, wipe out and not have to swim back to shore for your board.

OPPOSITE: **North Shore stretch.**

ABOVE: **Yes, surfing again – still!**

In search of a few empty waves close to home, a surfer (BELOW) takes the long walk down the cliff to Lunada Bay on Southern California's Palos Verdes Peninsula.

RIGHT: Surf explorers Kevin Naughton and Tito Rosemberg in southern Morocco, January '75.

The nascent travel adventures of the '50s, from the marathon coastal explorations of Bob Simmons to the first Makaha and North Shore beachheads, established a solid nomadic ideology. Bud Browne went wave hunting to Australia in the '50s. He was followed by Bruce Brown and the boys after they'd paddled the first surfboards into the waves of West Africa. A couple of years later, Englishman Rodney Sumpter toured the Ivory Coast and other West African environs. Then came the redoubtable team of Kevin Naughton and Craig Peterson

with their invincible Brazilian compatriot, Tito Rosemberg. Greg MacGillivray and Jim Freeman helped Mark Martinson and Billy Hamilton fill their passports with stamps in the '60s, making *Free and Easy* and *Waves of Change*. Dozens of moviemakers and magazine photographers began to tour the world with their surf stars, searching for the new spot – the perfect wave – that would sell tickets or magazines.

As the domesticated beaches of the world became more crowded, the surfari, or quest to find the undiscovered or uncrowded surf, became the essence of the surfing experience. The surfing magazines began to devote an increasing percentage of their editorial space to travel adventures, and continue to do so. From the humorous Griffin and Stoner travel adventures of the '60s (over the course of which Rick Griffin came of age as an artist and Ron Stoner found, then lost, his center as a photographer), to photojournalist Bernie Baker's groundbreaking (or was it surfbreaking?) surfari through Central America in the early '70s, to the delightfully scruffy tales of Naughton and Peterson's travels to Central America, West Africa, Morocco, Spain, France, Ireland, Mexico and Fiji, the contemporary jet-set world of surfing was pioneered by adventurous individuals with an itch for waves and wandering. But sometimes travel brought other, more illicit rewards.

The Boogie Board

Another milestone in the annals of saltwater democracy was the Boogie Board™, created by an engineer-turned-watertoy conceptualizer named Tom Morey, who bailed from Ventura and wound up on the Big Island. Morey was a man with a multitude of ideas. He designed boards with air intakes, multiple flutes, bizarre Neptunian outline shapes and all manner of odd fins and keels. He fantasized air-lubricated motorized boards that skimmed along on time-release sodium bicarbonate bubbles. His ruminations and illustrations appeared in *Surfer.* None of it was really gonna happen. But then something did.

He was living in Kona, his wife was pregnant and it was hot. "I had no money, and the surf was good right off the front yard, and I had some of this polyethylene foam in the garage – it was left over from doing the things for the Surfer article – so I got out the *Honolulu Advertiser* and then I borrowed an electric carving knife and an iron, and I cut out a little four-and-a-half-foot-long board with the knife, and then I ironed the foam [to seal it] with the newspaper in between, and the print of the newspaper transferred to the board, and that's how I know the date." It was July 7, 1971.

Morey paddled out; by now the surf was "crappy, but I could feel the wave; I could *feel* the motion of the surf, and here was this board with no fin just snakin' along." He nicknamed his new creation the S.N.A.K.E. for Side, Navel, Arm, Knee and Elbow, since he rode it prone, and all those body parts were picking up sensations of the wave. He ended up calling his new thing (in a smaller bodyboard size) a Boogie Board. It made an impact right away, especially with kids. Soft, light, small and ding-proof, it created a new kind of relationship with the ocean and made millions of people more intimate with waves.

The Boogie Board has proven to be the Volks-surfboard. It's gotten virtually every kid in striking range of a beach out into the waves. But Morey thinks that even now, some 25 years later, it's just beginning. "If you think there's a lot of people in the water now, you haven't seen anything yet. Someday everybody in the world will have a Boogie Board in the house. They're cheap, they're portable; you can take 'em to the pool, the river, the lake, the beach…and it's not gonna stop on this planet."

SURF CULTURE AND DRUG CULTURE

Marijuana had long been a common component of the driftwood-fire smoke at the beaches. Drugs came with the free-spirited mentality of the beach, and surfing's position on the cultural borderlands had long connected it to the beats and the bikers and other fringe dwellers. Surfing was always about freedom and experimentation, and the no-man's land of the beach was a good place to bring your bottle, your joint or your needle. Out on the sand, laws were laughed at, instructive signage was target material for paint or bullet, and the cops never came around because they just knew they were out of place.

There had always been cheap marijuana south of the border, but with the psychedelic revolution of the '60s and the soul-surfing era of the early '70s, demand for drugs had become huge in the United States (and elsewhere), and the surfers' nomadic lifestyle and free-spirited outlook put them in the right place at the right time to participate in some entrepreneurial ebb and flow.

In the early '60s, a California-based group of surfers who called themselves the Brotherhood of Light established one of the first organized drug operations, providing pure LSD, marijuana, hashish and other psychedelics to the surfing world. The Brotherhood was,

At first conceived as a sort of entry-level surf toy – a sort of Volks-surfboard – the Boogie Board™ was soon taken into the extreme surf conditions favored by bodysurfers, where the little boards' softness and flexibility made riding hollow waves in shallow water much safer. One of the greatest Boogie Boarders is Mike Stewart, shown above at Backdoor Pipeline.

Indonesia's Mystique

In the mid-'70s, Californian Bob Laverty looked down from a weather-diverted Djakarta-to-Bali flight and spotted the magic curving reefline 30,000 feet below in a remote national sanctuary called the Plengkung Forest Reserve. With Bill Boyum, he planned and executed the first recorded surf expedition into the place, utilizing Suzuki 80s as pack mules, traveling by ferry to Java and by bikes to Grajagan village. They loaded the bikes onto two primitive fishing boats to get across the lagoon to the reserve, then rode the bikes along the beach until they got bogged down in sand and coral. They proceeded on foot through the shoreline jungle, with its big cats and monkeys, and collapsed, exhausted, in the black of night. When they awoke they were presented with the spectacular sight of perfect six- to eight-foot barrels peeling from left to right for hundreds of yards right out in front of them.

Australian power-surfer Gary Elkerton blasts out of the barrel at G-Land.

"I want to have film of a surfer," Timothy Leary (CENTER) told Surfer publisher Steve Pezman in 1977, "moving along constantly right at the edge of the tube. That position is the metaphor of life to me, the highly conscious life. That you think of the tube as being the past, and I'm an evolutionary agent, and what I try to do is to be at that point where you're going into the future, but you have to keep in touch with the past ... that's where you get the power ... and sure you're most helpless, but you also have the most precise control at that moment. And using the past ... the past is pushing you forward, isn't it?"

in fact, a large network of investors, organizers, traffickers and dealers, but the people who were out there taking the big risks – getting their hands on the drugs in dangerous parts of the world – were often traveling surfers.

One prominent big-wave rider of the '60s – a smooth well-spoken young man – learned that smuggling was a good way to make a lot of money fast. On his first assignment, he and his girlfriend, posing as rich American newlyweds, flew first-class to Germany, purchased a new Mercedes, and made their way by road and ship – five-star accommodations all the way –

to Afghanistan, where they booked into Kabul's finest hotel. There, while they dined in high style, the car was taken from the garage, the rocker panels were cut and removed, the body was packed with hashish and hash oil, and the car was welded back together, sanded, perfectly repainted and returned before morning. The couple then left the hotel and continued their five-star honeymoon journey as far as Karachi, where they put the Mercedes on a boat bound for Long Beach, California, then took a taxi to the airport and flew home, first-class.

That was the easy part, the surfer says. Now he had to wait until the car arrived, cleared customs, and was ready to pick up. Only then, when he came for the car, would he know if they'd been successful. This was the beginning of a long, cautious and successful smuggling career.

In *Mr Sunset* (1997), Phil Jarratt recounts the life story of pro surfer Jeff Hakman, including the tales of a couple of harrowing drug-smuggling runs, beginning when he was a team rider for Plastic Fantastic, the hottest California surfboard brand of the psychedelic era. When Hakman discovered other team riders were importing hashish across the border from Mexico in "channeled" (hollowed-out) surfboards, he was persuaded to make a run, too. Although a crack in the fiberglass combined with the hot sun caused hash oil to ooze out of one of the boards, the border guards didn't notice, and they made it through OK. This perilous first attempt led Hakman into a couple of very heavy deals (including runs in Lebanon and Thailand), a bust, some jail time...and eventually heroin addiction.

The search gained momentum in the '70s and '80s. Dean Pinsak and Bobby Owens (TOP, LEFT) looking for waves in Morocco in '84, following those who'd gone for waves – and more – a decade earlier.

TOP, RIGHT: Rick Griffin helped paint MotorSkill for John Severson's *Pacific Vibrations* in 1970, then moved to Northern California to explore new regions of art and consciousness.

ABOVE: Deep into Mexico, California surfers found great waves and good pot (a false bottom in the WD-40 can hides the stash, c. 1976).

After several years of recession and apathy, the competitive scene gathered steam in the mid-'70s with the arrival of a new generation of surfer. Most of the important contests were held on O'ahu's North Shore. A typical 1975 lineup (ABOVE) featured Ian Cairns (Australia), Shaun Tomson (South Africa), Mark Richards (Australia), Terry Fitzgerald (Australia), Jeff Hakman (Hawai'i) and James "Booby" Jones (Hawai'i). These surfers rode longer, narrower boards in Hawai'i, where the waves were faster and more powerful than elsewhere in the world.

PREVIOUS SPREAD: The search is never-ending, the vagaries of swell and wind and tide create an ever shifting palette. Glen Campbell searches for green waves in New Zealand.

Things got pretty hot in Hawai'i back in the mid-'70s, and Hakman and associates weren't the only surfers in the thick of it. Boards packed with cocaine were coming in from Peru, then were being passed on to California. Thai pot was coming in, too, with servicemen from Vietnam or "vacationing" surfers. Maui Wowie and Big Island "bud" were also on the move. Hash, hash oil, opium and heroin had been coming through Hawai'i from Southeast Asia for many years, except now the surfers were getting involved, and it was having a noticeable affect on some major players. The greatest Australian surfer of the period, Michael Peterson, was working with a heavy drug habit, eventually retreating into institutional oblivion, as did *Surfer* magazine's great photographer, Ron Stoner.

It got uglier. Long Islander Rick Rasmussen, an early Bali surfer, was shot dead on a Harlem street corner while trying to score some smack. Small-time surfer-smugglers were suddenly cutting into lines of distribution they didn't even know existed. One night, a *haole* surfer was beaten on the North Shore, then tied to a chair and held at gunpoint while his girlfriend was raped by each of the assailants multiple times. Surfing was not looking entirely like a clean, healthy sport, and Hawai'i was starting to seem more like paradox than paradise.

As the action got meaner and the crowds got thicker, a few surfers started looking for other places to surf, and they found them. Everywhere. Deeper Baja and mainland Mexico, the Caribbean, South Africa, France, Japan, Bali, Morocco – it turned out the world had a lot more surf than anyone had expected.

MONEY FOR NOTHIN', CHICKS FOR FREE

The soul of surfing has always been in motion, but its heart has always been Hawai'i. There's just no better, more intense surf (not to mention the perfect climate and golden beaches of the highest order) anywhere on the planet. After surfing's early '70s dispersion, the sport quickly reestablished itself back home in Hawai'i and the North Shore, where the stretch of O'ahu coastline between Laniakea and Sunset Beach is often called the seven-mile miracle. Hawai'i remained the ultimate proving ground. Each winter surfers came from all over the world, and each winter many of them didn't go home. They became firemen, lifeguards, carpenters and roofers, teachers and fishermen, politicians and professional athletes. They did anything to remain.

In the early '70s, there were a couple of small shops on the North Shore – Country Surfboards in Haleiwa, later a small shop at Sunset Beach near Kammie's Market. Most boards were made in town but a lot were made in garages and sheds, too. With so much experimenting going on, surfers started to accumulate a collection of boards – a quiver designed to fit a variety of conditions – each board built for a specific range. Smaller, wider, curvier boards for smaller surf; longer, narrower, straighter boards for bigger surf. Every swell that hit the North Shore was both an expression session and a test drive. During contest season (roughly November through January), you could add to the mix the day-to-day pressure of several thousand of the best surfers in the world confined to a relatively small sandbox.

The early '70s winter sessions on the North Shore were dominated by the Hawai'ians – Jeff Hakman, Barry Kanaiaupuni, Jock Sutherland (back from domestic duty in the Army),

Mobility and lack of structure in the surfing lifestyle made for a convenient crossover from surf culture to drug culture, and a number of surfers have been survivors – or casualties – over the years.

ABOVE: **Rick Rasmussen.**

BELOW: **Jeff Hakman.**

The Hakman Connection

Jeff Hakman was the best competitive surfer between 1965 and 1975, from his win at the '65 Duke to his victory at the '76 Bells Beach contest in Australia, where he won in the throes of a heroin binge. It was after the latter event, in the town of Torquay, that he reached an agreement with Alan Green to license him and his business-minded friend Bob McKnight (with financial backing from McKnight's father) to distribute Quiksilver "board-

shorts" in America. The trunks' unique design (yoke-style scalloped legs and a wide waistband) was perfect for surfing and dovetailed with a strong surge of Australian influence in the sport to become the hottest thing in surf fashion, circa '76–'78. Hakman and McKnight made a pile of money, but Jeff had tried heroin in Bali the year before, and his addiction became the monkey that eventually rode him out of the company and nearly

out of surfing. He reestablished relations with both some 10 years later when he partnered up with Harry Hodge (the high-rolling freewheelin' filmmaker who made the film *Band on the Run* in the '70s) on the wildly successful boarding company Quiksilver Europe (aka Quiksilver Na Pali), with sales of $72 million in 1996.

Gerry Lopez

Always privy to the foibles of his surfing friends, Gerry Lopez never seemed to lose his focus or succumb. He kept himself in shape, practiced self-discipline and maintained his "center" while others struggled with temptation and lost. Born and raised in Honolulu, of Cuban-German-Japanese descent, Gerry grew up riding the waves around Waikiki, graduated to the North Shore and began to make an impression at age 20 in the winter of '68–'69. A calculating contest surfer, he did well and made the Hawai'ian World Contest teams in '70 and '72. But the real contest for him was the Pipeline, where he became the undisputed master of the barrel, establishing the tube ride as surfing's ultimate maneuver and the Pipeline as surfing's most perfect tube. A disciple of Dick Brewer's psychedelic Zen approach to surfing in the late '60s, Lopez soon found his own path. He was shaping for a company called Surfline in Honolulu when he and salesman Jack Shipley decided to start a new surfboard company, Lightning Bolt. Driven by Lopez's powerful charisma and talent, a loose confederation of independent surfer/shapers gathered under the Bolt emblem, which became the most powerful symbol in surfing in the mid-'70s.

Featured in three of the best surf films of the decade – *Five Summer Stories* (1972), *Hot Lips and Inner Tubes* (1978) *and Free Ride* (1978) – Lopez got to play himself in writer/director John Milius' 1978 treatment of Malibu as Greek tragedy, *Big Wednesday*. Milius, an old Malibu surfer himself, liked Gerry, and Gerry liked films, so he was next cast as Arnold Schwarzenegger's sidekick, Subotai, in Milius' 1982 comic adventure film, *Conan the Barbarian*. He also played a wise near-mute Dayak warrior opposite Nick Nolte in *Farewell to the King* (1989).

"The Dayaks are natives of Borneo," Milius explained in a 1992 interview. "They're masters of the jungle, yet Gerry was more graceful than them … more silent. He'd climb right up a nut tree and sit on a branch – he always appears to be moving slowly, but he's really quite fast.

And he learns so fast! Like in *Conan*, Gerry would be first to learn the swordsmanship, then he taught Arnold and the others. He's amazing, really. He can run 40 miles, swim wherever he has to." Says Lopez in partial explanation: "Surfing forces you to focus on the here and now… That's one of the biggest lessons for anyone. So many live in recollection and anticipation, but you've gotta be focused on where your foot's going right now."

A succession of surfers have mastered the challenging tubes of Banzai Beach to a level beyond peer to earn the title of Mr. Pipeline. First there was Phil Edwards, then Butch Van Artsdalen, then Jock Sutherland, and then Gerry Lopez, whose supreme wave judgment and eloquent precision reflected his total mastery of the place (SEQUENCE). Seeking out similar waves in other parts of the world led Lopez to Bali, Java and Fiji.

SPREAD: **Lopez at Cloudbreak, near Tavarua Island, Fiji.**

Gerry Lopez, Sam Hawk, Eddie Aikau, Owl Chapman, Tom Stone, James Jones and a rapidly maturing Reno Abellira. There were only a few stellar visitors, like Australian Terry Fitzgerald (the Sultan of Speed), South African Gavin Rudolph and Californian Mike Doyle.

By 1975, the scene began to shift as a group of Southern Hemi surfers came in with determination and plenty of attitude to stage a self-described "backside attack" at the Pipeline. They took on the biggest meanest waves with an aggression usually reserved for goofy-foot (right foot forward) surfers. The hot performers were the Tomson cousins, Shaun and Mike, from South Africa, and a school of Aussies – Peter Townend, Ian Cairns, Mark Warren, Bruce Raymond and the very unique Queenslander Wayne "Rabbit" Bartholomew, whose cultural guru at the time was David "Ch-ch-ch-ch-changes" Bowie. These guys were great surfers, not only at the Pipeline but also at Sunset and Waimea. In interviews and articles they reaffirmed that the only way you really prove yourself in surfing is to go to the North Shore and take off on the biggest gnarliest waves...and make it...and talk about it afterward. Fame! "Their dream," wrote *Surfer* magazine, "was of a world where all you did was surf; then the thing you loved became the thing you did. They called it professional surfing, and despite a grumpy soul-daddy backlash, their act changed the way surfers everywhere regarded themselves."

The effect these Southern Hemi rippers had on surfing was electrifying; they brought the color back into a soulfully understated sport, and with the color came the money and the attention and even more concentration on the North Shore. In the winter of '77–'78, director John Milius showed up to film the Hawai'ian segments of *Big Wednesday*. While the surf fad of the '60s had long died out (though it thrived worldwide in the heating-up skateboard scene) and the movie was no box-office bonanza, the vortex of energy Milius created on the North Shore had a galvanizing effect, and the movie's emphasis on the BIG wave created a subtle shift in the sport's development. After years of media domination by the expressive stylish surfers who excelled in small and medium waves, big-wave riders began to get their due, and even more surfers were drawn to the North Shore's winter surf.

OPPOSITE PAGE, TOP: **Eddie Aikau at Waimea Bay, 1978; no one else surfed huge waves with so much style.**

LEFT: **The Aikau family, one of the core local surf families on O'ahu. Eddie, crouched on the left next to brother Clyde, drowned while swimming for help when the modern voyaging canoe *Hokule'a* got into trouble in a storm in the Moloka'i Channel. The rest of the crew was rescued and the canoe salvaged.**

BELOW: **Eddie Aikau's memorial service drew hundreds of surfers, island residents, family and friends to the sands of Waimea Bay, where Eddie had been one of the all-time greats. A memorial big-wave contest, dedicated to Aikau, is held each winter – if, and only if, the waves reach 20 feet or above. The event is referred to by surfers as "The Eddie."**

ABOVE: **Crowds got ugly, burning a couple of cop cars, at the '86 Op Pro in Huntington Beach. Surfing finally made headlines in L.A.**

PREVIOUS SPREAD: **The successful marketing of surfing in the 1980s put surf company logos on the shirts of people all around the world, and surfing contests were drawing more of an audience than ever. Fans watch Oceanside contest from the pier.**

Big Wednesday also meant big business, at least bigger than the scale surfers were used to. With only $150,000 annual prize money in pro surf contests and fewer lucrative sponsorship deals available, the production of the film (in Costa Rica as well as Hawai'i) brought a new kind of temporary employment for surfers, photographers, lifeguards, shapers and peripheral personnel. Bud Browne, Greg MacGillivray, Gerry Lopez, Billy Hamilton, George Greenough, Ian Cairns and Peter Townend, Malibu golden-era surfer Denny Aaberg (co-author of the script with Milius) and a slew of others got into the project, and the enterprise became a valuable learning experience that opened the doors to later Hollywood involvement in surfing and the North Shore.

Surfing reentered the mainstream in the 1970s, thanks to ex-Malibu gremmie and director John Milius, in *Big Wednesday* (ABOVE LEFT, 1978) and *Apocalypse Now* (LEFT, 1979). The title *Big Wednesday* was already familiar to surfers who'd seen John Severson's 1961 surf movie. On the four-wall circuit, Bill Delany's *Free Ride* (1978) set a new standard for independent sports films.

SURF SELLS, THE CULTURE QUICKENS

By the late '70s, catalyzed by the brash Australian energy, the film *Big Wednesday* and a few widely distributed surf films such as *Five Summer Stories* and *Free Ride*, the sport of surfing started creeping back into style. Back in Newport Beach, California, where a number of surfwear companies and the many successful surf shops were located, surfers started to counter the Australian influence with bold, radical small-wave surfing and colorful wetsuits and clothes. Among the kids haunting Newport's "hottest hundred yards" of jetties and tubes was trendmaker Danny Kwock, who would become vice president of advertising and marketing for Quiksilver. Meanwhile, several other top surfers got into the rag business, notably Michael Tomson, who started Gotcha Sportswear; his cousin Shaun, who started Instinct, and Southern California shaper and artist Shawn Stüssy. In fact, the surfwear businesses were benefiting mightily from the surging popularity of skateboarding (thanks in large measure to the advent of urethane wheels and the highly visual hotdog maneuvers they made possible for pool, pipe and ramp skaters). The new young Boogie Boarders wanted surfwear, too.

Besides skateboarding, windsurfing and snowboarding were also starting to pump new blood into the surfing arena. Invented by a Malibu surfer, Hoyle Schweitzer, and his sailing buddy, Jim Drake, back in the '60s, the Windsurfer™ didn't find an immediate market in the United States, where the sailing surfboard was seen as neither fish nor fowl. But in Europe, where everyone had heard of surfing but few could surf, the Windsurfer™ spawned dozens of copycat manufacturers and an entirely new watersport industry, which finally

The boutiquing of surfing shifted into seriously high gear in the 1980s as wetsuits exploded into color statements and stickers covered everything in sight. The lowly surf shops, too, were revamped and upscaled, reflecting the new status of a sport that was starting to boast a pro circuit with a juicy pot of gold at the end of the rainbow.

burst into popularity in the United States in the late '70s and early '80s with the advent of short maneuverable boards designed to be sailed in the surf. Snowboarding, even more than skiing and the single ski, would emerge as the winter complement to surfing and surf culture.

The infusion of capital into surfing as a result of the growing success of the surf-based clothing businesses had a profound effect on everything in the sport. As those businesses grew, so did their budgets – for team riders, advertising, movies, videos, television productions and event sponsorships. Surfing's own subculture was in another major transition, and,

Simon Anderson and the Three-Fin Thruster

Modern surfing is a function of the modern board. The very short, very light, very positive (in terms of traction), blade-thin thruster-style surfboard of the '90s was first developed by Australian Simon Anderson in 1980.

"Gentle Giant" Anderson developed the tri-fins in an attempt to get better traction in a competitive universe dominated by smaller surfers on single- and twin-finned boards. The lateral resistance the three fins delivered was so positive that these very short, light boards could be ridden with one foot on the tail, directly over the fins, and, by keeping the body in a steady rhythm of twisting and torquing, a surfer could maneuver higher and deeper on a wave than ever before. At least this was the theory, and it proved itself almost immediately in 1981, when Anderson kicked off the new year with dominating wins in Bells Beach and then the Coke Contest in Sydney. The rest of the surfing world switched to thrusters even faster than it did to shortboards in '67–'68.

The surf zone was looking mighty different in 1985 than it did in 1965. Gone were the longboards and knee-paddlers; no one rolled the waves as they used to do in the old days, no more he-man board-denting death grips while trying to hang on at eight-foot Inside Sunset. Now the kids just gave a stiff leg thrust as the wave approached, pushed the sharply pointed nose down beneath the surface with a well-timed lunge and literally swam under the wave on the low-volume board, popping safely out the back. It was called the "duck dive." If the

wave was too big for a duck dive, the surfer just dove under and let the leash snap the board back.

The short light boards were so extremely maneuverable they were like skateboards; surfers were soon spending less and less time in the water and more and more time in the air. And since the thruster performed like a skateboard, the psychology of skateboarding moved inevitably and irresistibly into the ocean. Tentatively at first, and then with grand abandon, Hawai'ians like Johnny Boy Gomes and Californians like Davey Smith pulled off some stunning moves. But it was third-generation surfer Christian Fletcher who pulled out all the stops on every level and went off the chart with aerial stunts and functional reinventions of surfing,

created by following lines *suggested* by the waves, but not actually a part of the waves. His maneuvers were, to quote a phrase in a word, sick. On five-and-a-half-foot boards that weighed less than seven pounds, he was throwing inverted aerial moves and weird flights of fancy straight out of a skateboard park.

The Thruster changed the face of modern surfing once again; within a few months, most everyone rode one.

depending on how you looked at it, the right thing at the right time could – like foam and *Gidget*, shortboards and drugs – trigger some kind of reaction. The next thing to hit, the one that really launched surfing into the mega-sport/business it is today, was the three-fin thruster surfboard invented by Simon Anderson in 1980.

The attempt to create a professional surfing team occupied the efforts of **Ian Cairns** (CENTER) and **Peter Townend** (RIGHT) in the mid-'70s, but **Mark Warren** (LEFT) and **Cheyne Horan**, the other members of the Bronzed Aussies, weren't so blatantly committed. Cairns and Townend went on to start the National Scholastic Surfing Association and other projects designed to promote and teach surfing to a broader audience.

DUELING FOR DOLLARS

"These few Wall Street flesh merchants desire to unify surfing only to extract the wealth. Under this 'professional' regime, the wave rider will be forced into being totally subservient to the few in control in order to survive." [Mickey Dora, *Surfer*, September 1969]

There has, apparently, always been competition in surfing. Although paddling anchored the competitive format into the 1930s, when the sport regrouped at Makaha in the early '50s, wave-riding performance had moved onto center stage. The goal was to reward and honor the well-rounded waterman or -woman, with surfing as the most prestigious of the disciplines. Cumulative scores for surfing, paddling, tandem surfing and so on determined the champion.

More recently, surf contests are almost always *surfing* contests. Competitors are generally divided into divisions by age, sex and activity – menehunes, boys, juniors, men, masters, seniors, girls, women, tandem, paddle race, professionals – and any other divisions that make sense. As in other sports, there are also divisions by level. So surfing has a complex structure of local, regional, state, national and international competitions. This system was fairly well developed in the '60s, weakened in the '70s and recovered and intensified in the '80s and '90s, with forums for the contemporary surfboard and its polar opposite, the modern longboard.

By the late 1960s, nature-oriented "soul surfers" were advocating a slow-growth policy that resented the intrusion of contests into their surf spots. In a 1969 interview with *Surfer* magazine, Mickey Dora, already living much of the year abroad, reportedly scamming a living and on the verge of imminent full expatriation, said: "The advent of 'professionalism' to the sport will be the final blow. Professionalism will be completely destructive of any control an individual has over the sport at present." Professionalism is black!" chorused Santa Cruz local John Scott in a *Surfer* article.

Surfing changed as the money became too big to resist. It started out as a little – ($28 for "best ride" at the '62 Bells Beach Classic); then more and more – $2,000 for Terry Jones' first-place nose-time at Morey's second noseriding contest in '66; $300 for Corky Carroll's win at the first Smirnoff Pro-Am in Santa Cruz in '68; $2,000 for Nat Young's first place at the Makaha

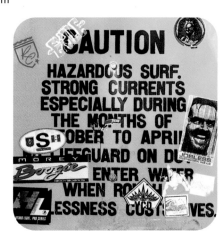

Surfing Contests have no authority without your Recognition disregard them.

SURFING CONTEST

Contest surfers interfere with us every day of the year Competition is a contagious virus injected by the media

Ban this Hostile take-over forever. wave riding lacks an immune system—without one The Wilderness Experience suffers.

no other sport typifies that Belief. "It isn't important if you win or lose..."

Competition makes the Rat Race run faster. Your Participation adds Momentum to it.

Boycott all contest sponsors

If it is illegal to have an open alcohol-container at the Beach, how can it Be accoptable to advertise at the Beach. Just say NO! Stop surfing under the influence. deprogramme yourself, de-pressurise Surfing only Hot Surfers can BURN cool surfers. Turn off The Radiation.

The crowd hates itself – with good cause. If you hate the crowd, Turn-off the crowd-making-machinery. Blackout the Media The ever-increasing crowds&hyper-aggressive Surfers are living proof that surf movies and surfing magazines cultivate crowds of well conditioned consumers It's time, make surf-photographer Pay. Surfers dont feel obligated to donate your day(s) demand pay

When it Becomes too dangerous and too competitive to enjoy riding waves, do you know whom to Blame? Blame yourself. Blame yourself if you allow Surf Photographers to use you as un-paid Stuntmen ego-feed is not Payment Blame yourself if you tolerate Being an un-paid extra Blame yourself if you buy Surf-magazines. Blame yourself if you attend surfing movies. Blame yourself if you support these parasites. If you recognise the problem, Be part of the Solution

Make Them Pay perhaps or make them go away

Deprogram yourself - de pressurise wave riding

If even 10 Surfers each day would demand pay $5.00 from all Surf-Photographers then either they would Pay or the conditions world-wide would begin to improve. You have the Right to do the Spot compensation otherwise you serve the media as a slave.

Smirnoff in '70; $3,000 for Michael Peterson's win at the '74 Coke Surfabout in Sydney; $1,000 total purse for the first Pipeline Masters in '71; and $130,000 for the Masters in 1996, with $20,000 going to the winner, Kelly Slater.

THE RISE OF THE WORLD SURF TOUR

Despite all the grumbling and anti-contest sentiment, it was clear that competition wasn't going to go away; the question was what form it would take. The vision of the time was tennis or golf – "If surfing could only be like golf," people were saying.

During December 1968, big-wave surfer Fred Van Dyke and television sports producer Larry Lindberg (producer of the televised "Dukes" for ABC) made a modest proposal to a group of top surfers gathered in Waikiki to become charter members of the International Professional Surfers Association (IPSA). The goal, in Van Dyke's words, would be "to establish a bona-fide world champion through a series of contests around the globe. We would also offer prize money, promote the sport and protect our members' interests." The model would be the Professional Golfers' Association (PGA). A number of great surfers signed letters of intent and Fred Van Dyke was elected president. Ron Sorrell, an Outrigger Canoe

While surfing purists like John Scott demonstrated their opposition to professional surfing's invasion of their local breaks, in this case Santa Cruz's Steamer Lane (TOP), other surfers enjoyed and profited from the emerging pro tour, in this case four-time World Champ Mark Richards of Australia, shown (ABOVE) being interviewed by Lord James Blears, the former wrestler and surfing enthusiast.

By the late '80s surfing was a big main-stream draw, and the Huntington Beach sands and stands were crowded with thousands of spectators for the annual U.S. Open Surfing Championships. Here, Hawai'ian star Sonny Garcia looks for a path back to the competitors' area after his heat.

RIGHT: Tom Carroll, two-time world champ from Australia, celebrates a Hawai'ian victory in '88.

FAR RIGHT: Surf signage in England shows significant cultural penetration.

Club member and a public relations executive, was named commissioner. Sorrell was convinced there was a future for professional surfing, and that future was on TV. Perhaps he was right, but the IPSA didn't last long enough to find out.

Fred Hemmings Jr. was at that meeting and signed a letter of intent. The '68 world champ had just counterpointed Scott's article in *Surfer* and wrote: "Professional surfing will identify our sport, improve all facets of competition, project a clean healthy image, and vastly improve and regulate the advancement of surfing techniques." Fred put his weight behind developing something he called the Professional Surfing Association. Fred knew there was a vacuum. He felt that without competition, no one who didn't surf would ever have any interest in surfing.

Surfing as Art

To some, the riding of waves is a religion; to others it's a sport – good healthy exercise and, they claim, nothing more. Some have said it's an ephemeral transient art form. If surfing is an art, perhaps it's a martial art, but in the spirit of aikido, the Art of Peace, using the opponent's own force to overcome.

This is the action of a man carving a surfboard on a wave: The wave tightens into a fist of power, the surfer moves into the barrel to greet it. The muscle relaxes, the fist opens and pulls back, the surfer slams off the wide-open face of the wave laying the shoreward rail of his board into a clean arc of beatific contempt. Bit much, eh? Well, from the perspective of the artist surfer, it's just a very beautiful thing.

The art of the dance, as personified by Gerry Lopez at the Pipeline on O'ahu's North Shore.

INSET: Expression is the name of the game in surfing. Matt Patterson at Huntington Beach.

The road to a successful world surf tour was rocky at best. The sixth World Surfing Championship (if you count the '64 in Oz, as surfers were now referring to Australia) was held in 1972 in San Diego. The anticipated rematch between David Nuuhiwa and '66 champ Nat Young never materialized, since Nat had retired to the land up at Byron Bay. Fred Hemmings, the '68 champ, didn't come, since he knew he didn't have a prayer in San Diego's small surf. Neither did Rolf Aurness bother to show up to defend his crown.

Nuuhiwa surfed brilliantly, having completely reinvented himself as a shortboard surfer, but the political winds seemed to be blowing another way, and there was rumbling from the local *hoi polloi*, too. His favorite board (a Fish design) was stolen, snapped in two and hung in effigy from the Ocean Beach pier with a good luck dave message scrawled on it. Apparently the locals at nearby Sunset Cliffs, who had developed the twin-tailed Fish, were feeling proprietary. On a borrowed board, Nuuhiwa outclassed the competition but lost the event. "I want to get drunk and forget about it," David said afterward. Such are the vagaries of judging a kinetic art form. In the dispirited San Diego backwash, the International Surfing Federation and the World Surfing Championship dissolved into dew.

Next Generation Curren

The California-born son of a notorious big-wave rider, Tom Curren quietly and methodically surfed his way up the amateur ranks as pro surfing was coalescing. A Christian lad of prodigious abilities, he twice turned down contest winnings to be able to surf in (and win) the resurrected (and now amateur) World Championship in Australia in 1982. He was signed by Ocean Pacific and advertised into the most well-known surfer of the '80s, even before winning his first world title in 1986. He won again in '87, got married and retired for a couple years, then came back to win again in 1990. He has been the subject of extensive media interest and was profiled by *Rolling Stone* magazine, was bold in his personal boycotting of South African events, dared to surf without sponsor logos on his board and preferred playing music to being interviewed. Since retiring from competition in the early '90s, he's remained a quiet and respected presence in the sport and a revered stylist, traveling the world in search of perfect waves.

Four years later, in September 1976, at the height of the new Aussie push, the International Professional Surfers (IPS) was founded by Hemmings for the express purpose of presenting the clean healthy sport of surfing to a mainstream audience. By retroactively recognizing existing events around the world, the IPS instantly created the pro tour that Van Dyke and Sorrell had visualized, plus it had its first world champion, Peter Townend of Australia, an excellent all-around surfer. Townend and his Bronzed Aussie buddy, Western Australian hottie Ian Cairns, buzzed around the world, surfing in every money event they could find. When the points were added up at year's end – *voilà!* – Townend was first (without winning a contest all year), Ian second! In a brief ceremony at the Outrigger Canoe Club, Hemmings snatched an old trophy cup from a shelf and presented it to a beaming Townend (for the camera), then set it back on the shelf.

Monumental snap-back by Tom Carroll (OPPOSITE) **on the way to winning his third Pipeline Masters title in 1991; total prize money for the contest was $100,000.**

ABOVE: **Three-time world champ Tom Curren cuts back to set up a tube ride at Off the Wall, a spot often referred to as Kodak Reef because it's such a perfect setup.**

It was a great gamble, but professional surfing now had a tour (and a legal way for a few talented individuals to make money). The purse for the 1977 circuit was already $146,000, and pro surfing – despite some ups and downs – never looked back. After a falling-out with Hemmings, Cairns campaigned for his new concept – the Association of Surfing Professionals – on a platform of self-rule in November–December '82. In a bloodless coup, the IPS and Hemmings fell, and the ASP (supported by dollars from Ocean Pacific, one of the most successful surfwear companies) took control of the world tour.

SURFING WAHINES

While a few women rode surfboards as early as the 1920s, surfing has remained a predominantly male sport in which macho misogynist bad-boy behavior has been elevated to the ranks of tribal ritual. From the '60s days of North Shore "barracks" helldates and Narrabeen clubhouse gang bangs to today's pro-circuit headbanger excess and "carnal-val" atmosphere, women have been virtually excluded from the inner circle of the sport. In the beginning, this was partly a function of the size and weight of the equipment; after a while it was a cultural mind-set, a men's club sort of thing. Even so, women surfed at Malibu in the '50s; even before Kathy Kohner, there was Vicky Flaxman, who, on that momentous trip to Windansea with the first potato chip boards in 1950, surfed the outside peak all the way to the beach and got a big round of applause from the guys.

The '50s, '60s and '70s saw a succession of outstanding women surfers – Marge Calhoun, Lynn Boyer, Joey Hamasaki, Phyllis O'Donnell, Sharon Webber and Joyce Hoffman (who won a lot of trophies, perks and press, but never a living wage) – but today's women surfers (beginning with Margo Godfrey Oberg, who parlayed her world championships into a lifestyle career as a teaching pro on Kauai, and Rell Sunn, "the Queen of Makaha"), are athletes of enduring stature in the sport. California's Kim Mearing, Australia's Pam Burridge, Pauline Menczer, Layne Beachley and a half-dozen other Aussies are women surfing at a new level, winning money and sponsorships while moving their sport much closer to the men's ... and attracting other women to surfing in the process.

Curiously, one of the most dominant professional surfers of recent years is a woman, Lisa Andersen. At 16, Andersen headed for California, leaving her mother a note saying she was going off to be the number-one surfer in the world. She went to Huntington Beach, California, asked Ian Cairns to get her into a National Scholastic Surfing Association contest and never looked

While 20th-century surfing has been primarily a male sport, there have always been excellent women surfers.

ABOVE: Four-time women's world champ Margo Godfrey Oberg on the nose at her Santa Barbara homebreak (Hammonds Reef) in 1967, the year before she won her first title in Puerto Rico.

LEFT: Margo went on to raise a family, working as a surf instructor at a Kauai resort. Kauai is also home to Malia Jones (OPPOSITE), a most impressive surfer, who shreds with the best of the men, '90s style.

Lisa Andersen

In an article in *Outside* magazine titled, "Gidget Kicks Ass" (November 1996), Martha Sherrill wrote: "Within the anachronistically macho world of surfing, respect comes when you rip like a man and act like it's no big thing. Two-time world champion Lisa Andersen is the first woman to pull this off, changing the way beach boys look at beach girls and bringing droves of young women to the sport."

At 27, Andersen toured the World Championship circuit with her three-year-old daughter, Erica, winning her third straight world title in 1996. The summer before, Andersen had competed in a specialty event on the men's World Championship Tour called the Quiksilver Pro. She was one of four women invited to join the 48 men in the jungle at the remote and dangerous G-Land event site in Java and she earned considerable respect from the male athletes by going for it in the big, grinding barrels, getting her face made over on the reef in the process. Andersen's dominance of the women's pro division is profound, and she is expected to equal or surpass the four-time-world-champion marks reached by fellow Floridian Frieda Zamba ('84, '85, '86, '88), South African Wendy Botha ('87, '89, '91, '92) and the illustrious ground-breaker herself, Margo Godfrey Oberg ('68, '77, '80, '81) – if she continues to tour.

back. After a short but stellar amateur run, she turned pro in 1987, ended the year 12th-ranked in the world and was named ASP Women's Rookie of the Year. Through the vehicle of surfing, in two short years Andersen transformed her life and achieved the aim that seemed so far-fetched to her mother.

THE GREEN SOUL OF SURFING

Environmental awareness had been growing within the surfing population since the mid-'60s, with the unsuccessful fight to save Dana Point from the Army Corps of Engineers (ACE). For longtime surfers, the giant breakwall is an ironic reminder of the glory

Lisa Andersen came out of Florida to become the most dominant female surfer on the world scene in the 1990s. At times traveling to international events with her infant daughter, she demonstrated a range of skills and a focused determination that put her on an equal footing with top female athletes in sports like tennis, track and golf.

Kelly Slater

Kelly Slater was another kind of phenomenon. From humble Florida origins, a torrid amateur surfing career in high school and a meteoric rise to world champion, Quiksilver's $1-million-a-year kid reigned supreme in the mid '90s in a way that has rarely occurred in the history of the sport. With spectacular good looks, a shy intelligence, a fearless abandon and a relentless need to win, he was a subject of fascination far beyond the limits of surf culture. Costar of the rave TV show *Baywatch* for a couple of seasons (until that scene was just too much, money or no), cover boy on *Interview* magazine in '95, featured in *People* mag's "50 Most Beautiful People," Slater was unabashedly trying to get as much out of surfing as he could without prostituting himself. He knew that, despite the resurrection of a lot of history and the honoring of its legends and heroes, this was still a young man's sport – and at 25, he could still apparently win whenever he wanted to. When seriously challenged, he just raised the level of his game. Whatever it took, he could usually do it.

ABOVE: **No other surfer of the modern era has so thoroughly dominated professional surfing as Florida's Kelly Slater. Proving himself in big Waimea at the 1996 Eddie was par for the course for this multiple world champ.**

INSET: **Slater with Bob McKnight (left) of Quiksilver, the surfwear company that paid Kelly a reported $250,000 a year to wear its threads.**

OPPOSITE, TOP: **When Eddie Vedder of Pearl Jam donated $50,000 to the Surfrider Foundation, he did it in front of a toilet because, he said, "that's what the oceans are turning into." Surfrider's *MOM* album showed broad-based support in the music world for protecting water quality in the surfing world.**

OPPOSITE, BELOW: **The essential experience underpins all the hype and hustle. Evening camp in Baja.**

days of Killer Dana, one of California's finest early big-wave spots. In the late '60s, a Save Our Surf movement began in surfing, initially over access issues, then in response to oil spills, proposed harbors, coastal development, the pollution of ocean waters and other issues.

One of the first things that surfer/shaper Steve Pezman did when he joined Surfer as associate editor in 1970 was to establish a new magazine department, "OMO" – Our Mother Ocean – a forum for environmental issues that is still actively maintained today. Replacing John Severson as the magazine's publisher in 1971, Pezman's persistence began to bear fruit, albeit indirectly, in the late '70s and early '80s when a a number of surfers became more active in their communities and environments.

In the late '70s, three Northern California surfers observed that a local fisherman was removing rocks from one of the reefs that produced the excellent waves at Shelter Cove and using them to build a breakwater to shelter his boats. One of the surfers, Tom Pratte, was a student of environmental studies at Cal State Humboldt; Pratte embraced the "deep ecology" philosophy that underpins radical environmental organizations like Earth First! and the Sea Shepherd Society. After trying various forms of friendly persuasion, then raising up public opinion against this illegal destruction of a natural reef area, Pratte was able to get the California Coastal Commission involved and, finally, stop the breakwater. Following several years of solo campaigning on this and other issues, Pratte landed a job as "the environmental guy" with the Western Surfing Association (WSA) and moved his focus to fighting the Army Corps of Engineers' draining of Malibu Lagoon, which was destroying the surf break. With persistence and keen research skills, a $3,000 grant from the WSA and ongoing support from foam magnate Grubby Clark, Pratte was able to make considerable headway in a number of areas, notably where ACE projects threatened coastal wetlands and surf spots.

Because surfing involves such intimate contact with the natural world at a time when most humans are increasingly sealed off in artificial surroundings, surfers have some responsibility for alerting others about any problems they become aware of in the ocean environment. As Bill Hamilton wrote in 1971, "Just by the fact that we ride the waves of the ocean, we are major responsibility holders to the future and [the] ecology of Earth."

Former world champ Nat Young has been quite vocal on environmental issues over the years and even ran for the Australian state parliament on an environmental platform: "With such a large number of surfers on the planet, I think we should be speaking from an environmental platform because that is where we're coming from," he said in a 1996 interview. "Longboarders, shortboarders, all of these people that add up to being members of this big tribe called surfing, we're all saying that these should be your priorities – number one, environment!

The Surfrider Foundation

Glenn Hening, a surfer and a computer specialist at Jet Propulsion Laboratory in Pasadena, wanted to create an organization that would give surfers a way to get involved in their communities. He hooked up with Lance Carson, "the most famous surfer I knew," who was vitally concerned about Malibu and knew Tom Pratte. This led to a three-way conversation that prompted Hening, in 1984, to found the Surfrider Foundation, surfing's first environmental nonprofit organization, and to shift the organization in a decidedly environmental direction. Pratte was on the board of directors and later served as Surfrider's executive director.

With financial support from Grubby Clark and founding members like Yvon Chouinard at Patagonia Inc. (who donated $10,000 for surf enhancement – artificial reef development – and some $65,000 overall in Surfrider's first decade), plus help from the surfing magazines (who ran free membership ads), Surfrider quickly became a presence in the surfing community. "Tom Pratte played a key role in establishing our credibility with his environmental research," says Hening, who left the group in '86. "I was like the booster rocket," he jokes; Hening continues to be involved in clean-water efforts and puts out an annual *Ground Swell Society* publication.

During Pratte's tenure, Surfrider joined San Francisco attorney Mark Massara in bringing suit against two Humboldt County pulp mills that were polluting Northern California surfing areas. Surfrider was eventually joined in the suit by the EPA (there were more than 40,000 documented violations of the Clean Water Act at the mills, operated by Louisiana Pacific and Simpson Paper Co.) and won its case in 1991, the second largest CWA suit in American history. "The paper mills tried to buy Surfrider off," Hening says. "'How much money for this to go away?' they asked us. We told 'em, 'We want clean water,' and they said, 'Sure, that's cute, but really, what will it take for this to go away?' And we said, 'We want clean water.'"

This and other successes (blocking break-waters at Bolsa Chica, Seal Beach and Imperial

Beach in California; restoring natural dunes habitat on the Outer Banks in North Carolina) and awards brought a lot of attention to Surfrider, which has attracted many nonsurfers to its board and staff and has garnered a lot of support. In 1995, surfer Eddie Vedder and his band Pearl Jam donated $50,000 to Surfrider "for their work to protect the oceans." John Densmore of the Doors donated $15,000 in 1996, and the organization's many "in kind" contributors include *Rolling Stone* magazine, MTV (at $50,000), the Surf Industries Manufacturing Association (SIMA), Interscope Records and Surfdog Records (at $100,000), *Wired* magazine and a

slew of other surfing and nonsurfing businesses and individuals. Its advisory board includes Patagonia's Chouinard, actors Woody Harrelson and Gregory Harrison, the Beach Boys and Mati Waiya of the Chumash people, the native inhabitants of the Malibu coast.

In 1996, Surfrider and Surfdog Records teamed up on a CD project called *MOM* (Music for Our Mother Ocean), which was gifted with original songs by such illustrious music makers as Beastie Boys, Jewel, No Doubt, Porno for Pyros, Pearl Jam and others and raised more than $200,000 for the organization. A second *MOM* effort released in 1997

features Dick Dale's "Miserlou '97." According to current Surfrider executive director Pierce Flynn, it's "Metallica meets Dick Dale."

By 1997, Surfrider, a grassroots-based non-profit environmental organization, had 25,000 members in 33 chapters in the United States and Puerto Rico, plus chapters and affiliates in six foreign countries, including France.

SPREAD: Surfrider protest paddle on the polluted Adour River in France was led by former champ Tom Curren.

By the 1940s, the Hawai'ian shirt was almost a Hawai'ian icon, along with the lei and the ukelele. President Harry Truman proudly wore a humidity-creased aloha shirt on the cover of *Life*, and Elvis was attired appropriately in *Blue Hawaii*. A curious side note: Hawai'ian print artist Keoni (John Miggs) designed a surfboard for kiddies in 1950, a four-and-a-half-foot-long wooden Hawaiian Surfboard – as he called it – with rollerskate wheels attached. This was a man ahead of his time, indeed.

SURFWEAR AND CULTURE SHOCK

Surf fashion began when the surfers who traveled to Hawai'i adopted the casual apparel of the tropics – aloha shirts initially, followed by Hawai'ian-style trunks – then returned home, where such apparel was, by definition, exotic. Actually, from a California or mainland standpoint, surfing itself was exotic. It was certainly fascinating in the pre–World War II years, then in the '50s and '60s it acclimatized in California, but only "sort of." Surfing always takes place "abroad" – in the boundary-less sea – and its cultural life is on the beach, that desert of ionized silicon dioxide, that no-man's land where people strip naked and just lie around and relax. It's all pretty exotic, and so is the culture that emerges. And that's what gives surfing its allure.

From its humble beginnings in the hand-painted or stenciled *tapa* (bark) cloth Hawai'ian clothes of the early 1900s (actually a synthesis of the American pioneers' Thousand Mile Shirt and the Japanese work shirt, called the *palaka* in the islands) to the silk, cotton and rayon (invented by Du Pont in '24) aloha shirts created for tourists in the '20s and '30s, the Hawai'ian shirt spearheaded the Polynesian surf-style invasion of staid European-inspired mainland attire. Out of the exquisite floral designs of Musa-Shiya (the Shirtmaker of Shoten), Elsie Das (Hawaiian Originals), John Miggs (aka Keoni of Hawai'i) and others, an industry was born. Kamehameha Garment Company Ltd. (founded by Herbert and Millie

Briner) and Branfleet (founded by George Brangier and Nat Norfleet), later Kahala, were the first to incorporate. Kahala's "pineapple tweeds" shirt was extremely popular in the '30s. Bearing the royal Hawai'ian crest and the motto "The life of the land is perpetuated in righteousness," the shirt was worn and endorsed by Duke Kahanamoku, for which he received a 50-cents-per-unit royalty, making him the first surfer sponsored by a sportswear company. The shirts were casually popularized by celebrities who wore them – Hollywood surfers Richard Boone and Peter Lawford at Waikiki with the Duke in '47, Harry Truman on a 1951 cover of *Life*, Montgomery Clift in 1953's *From Here to Eternity*, Arthur Godfrey on his mid-'50s TV show (he wore a new one every day), and Elvis in *Blue Hawaii* in '63.

Hawai'ian shirts became the basis of the surfer look and were – along with tailored M. Niis surfing trunks of the '50s – the foundation on which today's multibillion-dollar surfwear industry was constructed. This surfer style had a burst of popularity in the early

'60s, was eclipsed by the even louder statements of the psychedelic '60s and looked corny in the conservative backlash of the '70s when, especially in California, surfers took on the organic neutrality of seals or dolphins, wearing black rubber suits and surfing plain simple surfboards. But this couldn't last because so much of surfing wasn't just surfing, it was style, and style (to some minds) means fashion.

In the late 1980s, surfing came back with a vengeance, blasting into style across the United States like never before. In fact, it was the planetary convergence of three board sports (surfing, skateboarding and the rising star of snowboarding) that magnified the impact, creating a powerful nexus of radical image, insouciant attitude and contemporary street art that caught America's youth in midstride and swept them to the beach on the shifting winds of fashion. Sitting fat and happy, the more established surfwear companies were feeling cocky. "If you don't surf, don't start," imperiously suggested the first page of a Gotcha ad. "If you surf, never stop," advised the second. "Wave Attack!" "Surf Till It Hurts!" "Future Shock!" screamed the ads. Suddenly a Californian actor was in the White House and everybody wanted to be a punk surfer.

While the established surfwear companies that had survived the '70s and '80s ramped up for the long-awaited payoff, a rash of new companies jumped into the fray, each trying to "out core" the other with "authentic" phrases, looks and poses. The surf magazines swelled in size to well over 200 pages an issue (from a '70s standard of about 100 and an early-'80s average of a little more than that). The top brands of surfwear were snapped up by the big prestigious department stores, and product started pouring into the mass market like never before. Kids all over the country (and soon the world) were wearing Gotcha, Stüssy, Rusty, Quiksilver and Life's A Beach. "Surfing Is Life, The Rest Is Details," sum-

There is something in surfing that so perfectly fuses peace and danger, leisure and dramatic physicality, artful dance and contorted pratfall, so that the sport conjures the creative, the whimsical and the kooky like no other.

TOP: **Rick Rietveld's art captures the feeling.**

ABOVE: **The veteran feet of Mickey Muñoz with formal/informal thong options.**

LEFT: **Sticker shock, 1987, at the Newport Wedge.**

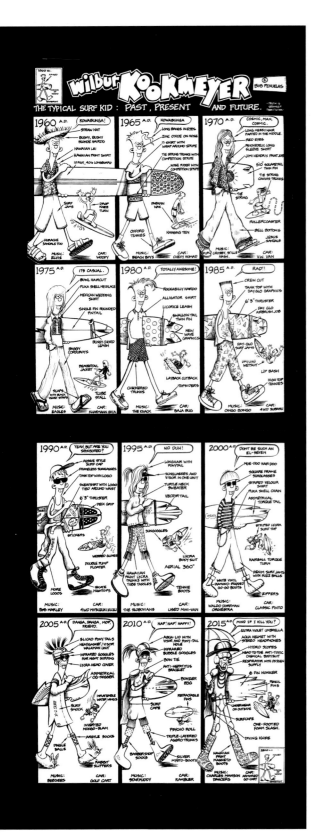

marized one ad for Instinct, and the rest of the world was starting to get the metaphor. Seizing the moment (as good surfers have been trained to do), dozens of surfboard manufacturers (skate and snow companies, too) hustled to shift their emphasis from hard goods to soft goods (clothes) in time to capitalize on the boom: Jimmy'Z, Billabong, Surf Fetish, Cruz, Pure Juice, Spot Sport European Beach, No Fear, Airwalk, Kozmik, Town & Country, Ooh Mau Mao, Maui and Sons, Local Motion, Mossimo, Island Magic, Island Scene, Hawaiian Island Creations, Bad Boyz, Local Boy'z, Newport Blue, Gordon & Smith, Body Glove, O'Neill and Hang Ten (founded by Duke Boyd in 1962) ... there were literally hundreds of them.

In 1990, Bill *(Free Ride)* Delaney's new film, *Surfers: The Movie*, opened to an enthusiastic surf press. Designed "to bring back the phenomenon of the surf film," it didn't fulfill the mission conceived by producer Michael Tomson of Gotcha, largely because the surf-video market was just taking off. *Surfers* was certainly the right name, though, because surfers were now in demand everywhere. Hawai'ian hunk Vince Klyn, weathering Aussie Nat Young, Ivy League–style islander Buzzy Kerbox, smoldering world champ Tom Curren and a dozen other "typical" image surfers were being sought after for prestigious fashion shoots in Hollywood, New York City or "on location."

THE CULT OF COOL

In a world where cool was becoming everything, surfing was now the cult of cool, and the commercial vampires wanted to sink their teeth into a big pulsing vein. The history and memorabilia and paraphernalia of surfing were all in big demand. *The New Yorker* ran a huge two-part article on the life and times of San Francisco surfer and cofounder of the Surfer's Medical Association, Dr. Mark Renneker, that was a great stereotype-breaker. Meanwhile, Christian Fletcher (head shaved, body pierced, tattooed) was short-circuiting the three top board sports into a new synthesis that would forever alter the subcultural character of all

three. In the middle of the late '80s rush (and between sessions with photographer Bruce Weber for Ralph Lauren), Nat Young described the moment for *Surfing* magazine:

"Surfing has been put across as a cult and it is a cult. I've been on this tribal thing for a long time. As a tribe, surfers are all after something the normal man in the street doesn't have a bloody clue about. I mean, surfers are becoming respectable now, a lot of people have put a lot of effort into that and that's great. But we *know* we're into something different." ["Surfers," November '89]

Surfing was now pop culture in a big, big way, and it had pragmatically adjusted its own culture accordingly. The complex character that Rick Griffin's cartoon Murphy had become (innocent gremmie turned mystic peyote-droppin' seeker turned born-again Christian) was replaced in the pages of *Surfer* with the clever but demographically low-pitched headbanger surf goon Wilbur Kookmeyer. The magazines, especially *Surfing*, adjusted their marketing to fit the target audience of the rag merchants – young males 12 to 18 – because they were the ones who spent the bucks. In 1989, *Surfer* launched *Beach Culture*, a magazine that celebrated the cutting edge of surfer style and its various influences and cross-pollinations.

Although the surf market sagged once again in the early '90s, it rebounded substantially in '94–'96. The small surf companies started by novice surf entrepreneurs of the '70s were no longer small. Quiksilver was up over $150 million in '95, No Fear and Op were crankin' at more than $120 mil, Gotcha, once at the head of the pack, was back up to a respectable $60 million and Rusty was over $40 million. With projected gross sales of $50 million in 1997, Billabong USA licensee Bob Hurley announced that surfing was cool again; one of several companies marketing new zipperless wetsuits made possible by improvements in foam technology, Billabong was one of a dozen companies that were able to afford a stable of top ASP (and other) team riders.

The more things change, the more they stay the same.

OPPOSITE: **For better or worse, Bob Penuelas' Wilbur Kookmeyer was the Murphy of the '90s. Future Quiksilver principal Danny Kwock** (OPPOSITE, RIGHT) **and the Newport kids used color to call attention back to Southern California in the mid-'80s.**

ABOVE: **Whitey Harrison's granddaughter, Coco, led the retro scene as interest in classic woodies led to big car shows and heavyweight price tags in the '90s.**

Big Money, Bigger Dollars

The big money coming into the sport via the sportswear companies meant bigger money for sponsored surfers. It was a dream that had been pursued since the Bronzed Aussies and even before. Corky Carroll was writing "professional surfer" on his tax returns back in 1965, when he was on the Hobie team. But the most Carroll claims to have made was about $40,000 in 1968, when his was the most recognizable name in surfing (he still ranks high in recognition, thanks to his round of Bud Lite commercials in the '80s ... and maybe for his *Surfer for President* album in 1980). Champion surfer Joey Cabell made a good pile of money, but that was as a founder of the Chart House restaurants (he still owns the one at Ala Moana near Waikiki). Although he was photographed on Sunset Boulevard by rock photographer Norman Seeff for the cover of *Surfing* in 1979 and looked plenty flashy in his silver Porsche, four-time world champ Mark Richards never made anything close to what surfers were making in 1995. Chris Carter, who was a senior editor at *Surfing* in those days, made a fortune, too, but that was as the creator and producer of "The X-Files" and other television projects. In the 1990s, marquee performers could run a successful surfwear company a cool $250,000 each, a price that's not unreasonable, according to Gotcha's Michael Tomson, who told reporter Matt Warshaw, "My theory is that 50 percent of all advertising and promotions are a complete waste of money — but nobody knows which 50 percent." ["Green on Blue," *The Surfer's Journal*, Fall '96]

As surfing gained momentum through the '70s and '80s, the top dogs experimented with power. Corky Carroll (ABOVE) reinvented himself as a guitar-pickin', folk-song singin', Bud Lite drinkin' Surfer for President. Gerry Lopez became chairman of the board at Lightning Bolt, and Mark Richards (SPREAD) drove a silver Porsche 911 up and down the east coast of Oz proclaiming wordlessly that professional surfing had arrived.

Surf shops, too, had progressed far from their low-rent roots; the surf shops of the '80s and '90s were slick lifestyle operations selling *da kine* gear for full pop. But the boutiquing of surfing had been going on for decades. That old bar of Parawax that was good enough for traction in the '50s became Surf Research's Waxmate in the '60s, Dr. Zog's Sex Wax in the '70s and Big Pecker Surf Wax by 1990, and by then most kids were applying AstroDeck or similar cushioned traction pads to the decks of their boards anyway – to cushion the shock of landing those aerial maneuvers. The beaver-tail jacket and long john wetsuit of the early '60s had bloomed into a highly sophisticated rubber market, with the original folks hell-bent on staying ahead of a determined pack of newer players. All of the new suits were leagues ahead of the best 10 years earlier – lighter, more flexible, warmer – making it easier to surf in them. Sunglasses, too – that's a universe of its own, with giant Oakley one of many successes.

The rising tide of surf culture sloshed over America and much of the rest of the world in the mid-'90s like a big Southern Hemi swell. SIMA numbers showed almost 2 million surfers in the United States in 1997, with more than 400,000 surfboards and almost

After watching windsurfers and skateboarders getting "massive air," a few brave surfers began to develop aerial maneuvers. Point man in the new air force was Christian Fletcher (OPPOSITE), shown in the summer of '89 at Trestles, which was now a California state park.

TOP: Surf contests are major events in Santa Cruz, thanks to blufftop spectator seating.

ABOVE: *Beach Culture* magazine staked out the fringes c. 1990.

600,000 wetsuits sold annually. Bruce Brown came out of cinematic retirement to create *Endless Summer II*, reflecting the times in its bipolar stars, Pat O'Connell, a hot 20-year-old shortboarder, and Robert "Wingnut" Weaver, a hot 26-year-old longboarder. As mystified over what surfing's all about as ever before, *Chicago Sun-Times* film critic Roger Ebert wrote: "The movie is wonderfully photographed. Right at the beginning, we see fabulous shots of waves and surfers. Some of the shots even go inside the 'barrel,' so we can see the wave curling over the head of the surfer. What a way to get stoked. These are terrific shots. We see them again, and again, and again. The operative word in the title is endless, not summer."

And he could be right. It *is* endless. The waves just keep coming, and now that the secret's out — that most anyone can paddle out and catch a free ride — well, there's no turning back this tide. It'll have its highs and its lows, but the roots of this sport and its culture have taken a firm hold in the energized coastal terrain, where daily exposure to billions of sprung ions has the power to transform dazed victims of contemporary lock-step society into healthy human beings with a historical legacy and a sparkle in their eyes.

Human nature is composed of a complex web of characteristics, drives and fears; these are reflected in man's pursuits. In surfing, the phenomenon of localism mirrors a conflicting maze of territorial imperatives, which are generally dealt with out in the water.

ABOVE: **Establishing priority from the get-go.**

OPPOSITE: **The arena and the pecking order.**

RIGHT: **A brash attitude, a ready grin and a flashy repertoire tend to pay off — they certainly have for the Fletcher clan (Christian, Herbie, Nathan and Debbee).**

FOLLOWING SPREAD: **From grommets to surf stars — who could have predicted (back in 1987 when the photo was taken) that one of these hot little surfers would become the most successful professional surfer of all time? Left to right: Mattie Liu, Sean Slater, Walt Cerney, Shane Dorian and Kelly Slater.**

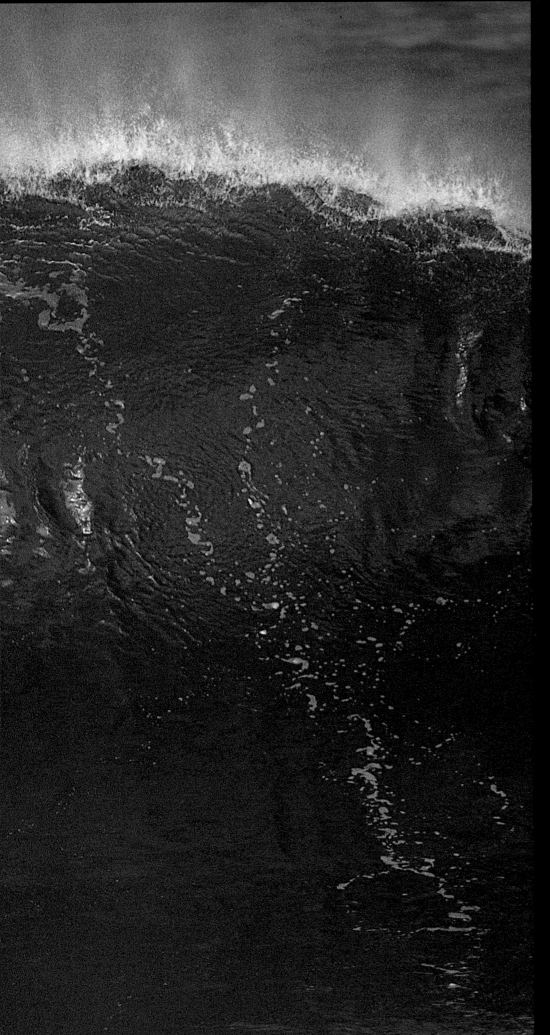

The Power and the Shark

One of surfing's most pithy aphorisms: "Waves are measured in increments of fear." The allure and danger of riding big surf is a defining dimension in surf culture. In general, the better a surfer becomes, the larger and more powerful and exciting the waves he seeks to ride. Eventually this takes a person very close to the edge of his physical abilities. A surfer may have all the knowledge and technique and strength to ride a 30-foot wave, but what if he makes a mistake?

Death by drowning is an image and a possibility that is always present in the surfer's mind. You're far out to sea, you've lost your surfboard, there's nowhere to stand, and you're cold and deathly tired. Of course, even when the waves are not life-threatening, even on those idyllic afternoons of small fun waves and perfect warm weather, there is always that remote possibility of...an encounter with...the landlord, the man in the gray suit. Although there have only been about 30 shark attacks on surfers in California since 1970, the close calls come frequently enough to stimulate the topic in the minds of the imaginative.

Nearer my God to Thee: Surfing is an "edge" sport to the extreme – racing the edge of a folding wave at the edge of the world, above the sharp edges of reef, with the living knowledge that, at any time, you can get a visit from the landlord.

SPREAD: **Bailing at the Pipeline.**

INSET: **From the Frog House wall in Newport.**

CONTEMPORARY CORE

"And now it's a graying demographic that's become ready to look back and romanticize its youth. With all the collectibles and all this stuff now, it's definitely not a hula hoop – it's a market, an industry, it's a sport, it's on television, it's got a lingo which has changed with the eras, it's got a $5.5 million circuit, it's got books, it's got authors, it's got magazines – jeez! – it's got a history." Steve Pezman, publisher of *The Surfer's Journal*, 1997 interview

Surfing is the ultimate metaphor for life. It accurately describes the way things happen: Life really is a wave, and your attitude is your surfboard. A situation – any opportunity – comes to you like a wave. And you are the surfer. You can't act before the situation develops, and you can't act after it passes. You can act only at the peak of the moment, where the energy is concentrated. You can play the metaphor at any level and, like surfing, with any style. You can surf with a hostile aggression or with a blank Zen mind. You can work at it and push yourself against your limits hour after hour, or you can make it a rich sensual experience – the beautiful, luscious, curling barrel muscle inviting you to penetrate and work your stick around inside (that sort of thing). A wave is a clear slate and a living mirror. Beach culture is what's reflected off of it. Surf culture is stepping through the mirror.

Few realities are so strikingly at odds as the land and the sea.

OPPOSITE: **Out of the water and into the arms of adoring fans, celeb Slater wades into the shorebreak after a Huntington heat.**

ABOVE: **The silence of the dolphins – Mark Cunningham, North Shore lifeguard and bodysurfer extraordinaire.**

When the cyberspace cadets started in with their "surfing the Web" stuff, the collective unconscious was unlocked in some big way. Suddenly it's clear that everybody in the world (virtually) wants to be a surfer – or understands that they are surfers.

On the eve of the millennium, images of surfers are everywhere. On one television commercial, the metaphor curls home as a cool band of longboard professionals in three-piece suits with attaché cases catch a beautiful curling brick-and-asphalt wave down Wall Street. In the early '90s, *Esquire* ran a photo spread on wetsuited corporate executives ("Chairmen of the Board" and "Surfin' MBAs") with the cover headline "Welcome, Chalk People, to the Coolest Scene in America" (*chalk people* being any nonsurfing fair-skinned inlanders). Four-time world champion and short-term *Baywatch* television star Kelly Slater pouts under a

A growing number of surfers are arming themselves with the technological toys required to tow one another into the giant waves that break on Hawai'i's outer reefs. This is the Maui JATO (jet-assisted take-off) crew, including Laird Hamilton, Gerry Lopez and several windsurfers with appetites for riding the huge waves at Jaws, the most famous strap-surfing spot (note the straps on the surfboards).

OPPOSITE: **Surfing's new image – later on Interview.**

white Stetson on the cover of *Interview* magazine ("Half Fish, Total Dish"), and *Baywatch* (that's surfing's seminal Santa Monica Bay) is just about the most popular syndicated TV show in the world. Daniel Duane's *Caught Inside: A Surfer's Year on the California Coast*, Kem Nunn's *The Dogs of Winter* and Richard Nelson's *The Island Within* received critical acclaim, bringing surf culture into national bookstores.

OVER YOUR HEAD

The difference between cybersurfers and real surfers is obvious. Cybersurfers do it in their heads. Surfers get in over their heads. It's easy. You paddle out, you're over your head. A big set comes, you're over your head. You get hurt, you're over your head. You're a half-mile out to sea and you're pointing down the heaving wall of a legitimate 40-foot waveface, and the wind coming up the face is blowing so hard your cheeks are flapping, and the water's sucking up the face, too, like down a storm drain, and you're not going anywhere... except... over... the... F-A-A-A-A-A-A-A-L-L-L-S-S-S, and you're way over your head. In fact, you're weightless, but your feet have already been whipped out of the straps. Then you're definitely falling, splattered around by God's own firehose, tumbled until you're stunned all over and

Surfing the Web

A recent search of "surf" using the Yahoo!-brand Web browser came up with 25 categories and 1,163 Websites using the word *surf* in some form.

The Websites included: the "post-punk power pop trio" Nada Surf; Club Ed: the Surf Coaching Professionals ("All Club Ed students are guaranteed to stand up and ride waves!") located in Santa Cruz, California; Surf Gate ("The purpose of this home page is to provide an Internet presence for area churches and Christian owned and operated establishments"); Surf Flite ("manufacturer of skysurfing boards and wakeboards; also have instructors that provide training for each of these disciplines"); Surf Sites for CyberBiologists ("comprehensive but not overwhelming selection of sites useful for novice cyberbiologists, who want to surf the biological dimension of the Web"); Yahoo! Surf Shop (T-shirt and other product sales); Frank Sussman Co. ("For those of us with high standards, a thirst for action, a lust for comfort and an eye for fashion, we introduce the RISE line of surf wear. It's righteous active wear for all occasions!"); Yahoo!'s own Surf

College Shopping Network
The Ultimate Shopping Adventure

The hottest site to offer unique and brand-name products at low discount prices. You can also browse for free games, entertainment, and scholarship links. Surf on for cool fun and shopping!

Let's go Surfing!

School (features "How to Surf," "Surf Guru," "Surf Lingo" and "Surf Stories," none of it related to water); Big Surf Cyber Cafe ("occupies real & cyber space. Refreshments, one dozen computers, both Mac & PC as well as a T1 connect server. Entertainment and shopping"); Ready, Aim, Surf ("professional links for librarians"); Surf Report ("statistical reporting program geared toward marketing professionals"); Cyber Surf Wear ("casual apparel for the entire family, featuring T-shirts and sweats"); Surf Cincinnati Waterpark ("over 10 waterslides and attractions. Harbor Club banquet facilities,

miniature golf, gokart racing, and bumper boats"); Skrank ("free Web-zine including surf, skate, snow, sound, sex. Hottest strippers, surfers, etc. No fancy, long wait crap – just the cutting edge interviews & graphics!"); M.I.R.V. ("San Francisco's industrial surf opera band on Poison Eye Records"); Blues Crazy Moon and the Sun Worshippers ("blues-inspired surf-a-billy lounge tunes to tickle your ears"); the Smooths ("Check out the only official Web site for the Smooths, a band which mixes the sounds of ska, surf punk, and disco"); Surfing the Self ("personal online advice from two psychologists"); Surf Touch Software ("produces touch-screen Web browser, and other touch-screen-based Web applications like Surf Cash"); and so on. Several hundred of the sites are actually connected with riding waves. But it's mind-boggling, isn't it? The biggest technological shift in some time, and the descriptive technical language is … surf talk. Let's go surfin'! Click-click.

blacking out until you somehow break the surface to gulp some oxygenated foam and hear the closing growl of a...motorcycle. Then you see the next monster walling toward you, already feathering into white at the top, and you turn to see the WaveRunner™ carve past, your partner tossing you a line. You grab it and hang on as he bottoms out the throttle, dragging you behind like a dead seal, blasting over the shoulder of the most giant wave you've ever seen, just in the nick of time. That's a good wipeout, tow-in strap-surfing style. Psycho style. Hero style. No-big-thing style.

Big surf has long been one of the siren calls of the Hawai'ian Islands, but the inherent challenge of riding the biggest waves, combined with the recent attention and publicity that comes with the territory, has conspired to increase the traffic and the danger. A new Baja big-wave discovery, Todos Santos, had been attracting big-wavers since the late '80s, but even Todos was soon getting crowded on the best days. Meanwhile, up in cold-water country, Northern California surfer Jeff Clark had been solo surfing the giant peaks off Pillar Point

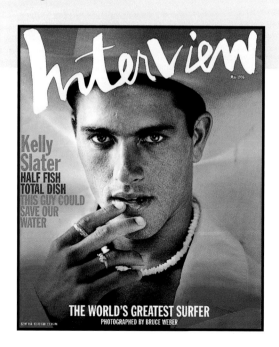

interview

May 1996

Kelly Slater
HALF FISH
TOTAL DISH
THIS GUY COULD
SAVE OUR
WATER

THE WORLD'S GREATEST SURFER
PHOTOGRAPHED BY BRUCE WEBER

The renewed fascination with riding significant waves comes with risks.

SEQUENCE: **Mark Foo's last wave at Mavericks; although not especially huge, the wave was utterly fatal. Below: Donnie Solomon met his end at Waimea Bay in 1995.**

OPPOSITE: **Outer Reef pioneer Alec Cooke (aka Ace Cool) barely escaped the ocean a few years earlier.**

for several years before a few friends dared to join him…and then the word got out that it was a heavier wave than Waimea. So the big-name big-wave riders had to come see for themselves, and that's how it happened that expert surfer Mark Foo, after surviving years of giant surf on the North Shore (and one historic 45-foot close-out wave at the Bay), dove off his board while dropping down the face of an 18-footer at Mavericks (December 23, 1994) and was discovered a couple of hours later, drowned at the end of his surf leash. Dozens of waves were ridden while Foo, who'd flown in from Hawai'i on the red-eye the night before, floated in the unfamiliar cold green water – bigger waves, ridden by less experienced surfers – but it was his time, friends said later. At least he died doing what he loved.

With more surfers riding bigger waves, the whole thing is starting to get into that spooky realm known as "statistics." You know, "If 1,000 surfers ride 100,000 waves over 20 feet, there's a 50-50 chance that 0.2 percent will drown. If the waves are over 25 feet, 0.8 percent will drown"…that sort of thing. When experienced big-wave rider Donnie Solomon died at Waimea a year after Foo (to the day and the hour, December 23, 1995) that was a little spooky, but when big-hearted 28-year-old North Shore veteran Todd Chesser drowned on February 13, 1997, at Outside Alligators (near Waimea), caught inside and held under by a big set, it seemed ominously statistical.

"In recent years, Chesser was finding it more and more difficult to stay ahead of the crowds," wrote *Surfer* field editor Ben Marcus in his report on the incident, "and he watched with growing depression as his happy hunting ground, the outer reefs, swarmed with serious big-wave surfers and tow-in wannabes. In the past year, Chesser had even discussed the unthinkable: moving away from the North Shore for good. He was engaged to a California girl and looked forward to … a normal adult life on the mainland…. A few days after his nightmare experience, Cody Graham [who survived the same set and had tried to save Chesser] had had enough: 'I'm over it. I quit. I left my big-wave board at the beach that day and just

The big-wave and outer-reef playgrounds are on a different scale – far more powerful and vast than the playful hotdog waves of Malibu, for instance.

BELOW: **Derrick Doerner goes bug-eyed as an obese Waimea lip prepares to whomp.**

OPPOSITE: **Sea Doo® pilot Dave Kalama has just towed Laird Hamilton into this Jaws wave and is racing toward the recovery position.**

FOLLOWING SPREAD: **Laird Hamilton in the straps at Jaws. This is truly theater of the extreme.**

walked away. Todd Chesser was solid as a rock. He was one of the fittest men on the North Shore. I don't know why he drowned and I didn't. I came that close to going with him. I quit.'"

"I think that they're towing themselves into waves that are bigger than man can survive in," says John Severson. "A lot of people are gonna die because I know, from personal experience, there's only so much that you can stand. There's only so long you can stay down, in the best of shape...but I think it's just incredible! To come down one of those big waves and see that wall in front of you pitching out, blocking out the sky...and making it! But you don't have any options if you make a mistake, and it may be your life. But life's getting cheaper; there's a lot of us."

The decline of the aloha spirit in the day-to-day life of surfers and surfing is an ominous indication of trouble at the heart of the sport. But all around the world there remain core pockets of surfers whose essential relationship with the waves and each other is also fundamentally sound, as honorable and joyful as the first surfers spotted by Captain Cook or Jack London.

SURF EXPRESSION

A subculture is in part defined by its language. In the beginning, a *gremmie* was a gremlin, a mischievous troublemaker and not truly a surfer. But then the term became one of affection, almost, and when the Australian influence swept in out of Torquay and Sydney, suddenly they weren't gremmies, they were grommets. It's a language that is always stretching, for at least three reasons: to describe new territory, for subtribal differentiation and due to outside influence (the cultural walls are quite permeable, and as much likely flows in as flows out).

Surfers today talk of "ramps," "ollies," "shack time," "schralping," "barneys" and an entire lexicon of general and specific terms that are more or less meaningful depending on your proximity to the subculture, or the sub-subculture. But the language includes the experience – the small acts and the big moves, the lifestyle accoutrements, the surfboards and the art. The language includes the images of a pantheon of photographers,

In the 1970s, surf art entered a golden age in which the meeting of man and wave inspired expressions in virtually every medium imaginable.

ABOVE: **John Casper demonstrating the shaper's art in Huntington.**

RIGHT: *Surfer* **founder John Severson's "Discovery" celebrates the search for the perfect wave.**

OPPOSITE: **"Trestles" by Ken Auster, whose photo-based watercolors are found in many Chart House restaurants.**

from Blake to Ball to Brown to Maki to Grannis to Stoner to Brewer to Wilkings to Divine to a hundred hot triggerfingers (and eyes) at work every day, building the dictionary of surfing's visible vocabulary. And the language includes the narratives, the words, of everyone from Cook, Twain and London to Matt Warshaw, Phil Jarratt, David Parmenter, Nat Young, Dora, Stecyk and a thousand more eloquent articulators of the sublime and the ridiculous.

The language includes all the places, too, from Waikiki to Malibu, from G-Land to J-Bay, from Gilgo Beach to Johanna. And the vehicles: *olo* and *alaia*, plank and cigar box, Hot Curl and Malibu Chip, pop-out and custom, elephant gun and noserider, vee-bottom and mini-gun, twin-fin and thruster, shortboard and longboard.

Three artists' visions of stoke:

ABOVE: **"Surf City, Here We Come" by California painter Lynn Coleman blends sun, surf and satiric wit in a raucous display of color.**

PREVIOUS PAGE AND BELOW: **Russell Crotty sketch of a tube-ride sequence beautifully captures the energy and nuances of the intense surfing experience.**

OPPOSITE: **Steve Valiere's "Stoked!" embroiders a moment familiar to all surfers – that first glimpse of the surf.**

Surfing has inspired a surprising number of artists whose creativity has been a synergistic companion to the wave-riding phenomenon. From John Severson, whose early cartoon work in *Surfer* emerged into idealized tropic psychedelia, to Rick Griffin, whose incredible illustrations took him to fame outside the surfing world, to Bill Ogden, whose neo-nouveau lines and '60s themes brought life to *Surfer* ads, to Caroline Zimmerman's moody landscapes, to Rich Rietveld's surreal airbrush creations, to Ken Auster's *plein-air* interpretations of classic surf photos, to Jessica Dunne's Hopperesque canvases – the list goes on and on.

Surfing in the 1990s has reached a level of sophistication that Duke Kahanamoku would have found unbelievable, but perhaps enjoyable. A full range of surf magazines (including the exquisite *Surfer's Journal* and the 'bout-time *Wahine*) have become guidebooks to the global surfing network, and surf camps at hot tropical surf spots (the one ABOVE is at G-Land on Java) have redefined the surf safari.

Clearly, the experience of surfing is stimulating, continuously evoking the artistic vocabulary of the surfer and the near-at-hand. The work of so many artists suggests why some surfers argued that wave riding was an art, not a sport, back in the early '70s.

And of course, there are the names; they're part of the vocabulary, too: Duke, Freeth, Blake, Whitey Harrison, Hoppy Swarts, Grannis, Simmons, Quigg, Velzy, Dora, Yater, Doyle, Dewey, Lance, Corky, Butch, Wally, George (and George, because, in the surf culture, there are at least two Georges), Peck, Morey, Midget, Nat, Cooper, Jacobs, Curren (the dad and the two sons), Archy, Joyce, Joey (two males and a female), Fain, The Surf Star Formerly Known As Kong, Buffalo, Rabbit, Buggs, Margo, Shaun, Owl, McTavish, RB, BK, PT, MR, Kelly and Lisa, and on and on, like some kind of strange living sea scroll.

While the vocabulary of surfing includes the literature and lore promulgated in books and magazines, the surf culture remains a substantially oral tradition, its information passed on at the beaches and out in the lineups, its tales told around evening campfires or in restaurants or bars after grueling sessions or in the midst of insufferably long lulls in the surf.

STATE OF THE ART

Today, there are surf camps – comfortable though spartan retreats within hailing distance of many of the world's great waves. There are new kinds of surfboards (notably built by Patagonia in Ventura and by Randall French in Santa Cruz) that use advanced composite technology to create longer-lasting, more environmentally sound surfboards. There are surfboard auctions where boards built with the old technology (those '50s and '60s longboards) go for $2,000 or $3,000, and an original mint hot curl might bring 50 thou. Dale Velzy, typical of the old shapers in new demand, is making 15 boards a week (from start to finish,

It all started in 1969 with Big Surf in Tempe, Arizona. Now there are "wave pools" around the world, some of them producing waves capable of hosting professional contests, like this one in Allentown, Pennsylvania.

The Stoke

Surfing ocean waves is exquisite play, and the surfers who ride them plug into a whole different reality, one that is so experiential that, naturally, words fail to describe it. How could anything of a play-nature be better? You're riding curling echoes of ocean winds and storms. You're cavorting in perfect spiralling three-dimensional laid-on-their-sides little tornadoes – skating down the zippering wall of the tube – in the center of the cyclone. Havin' fun.

As Nat Young once wrote: "Riding waves daily or consistently and taking it seriously enough, you run the risk of becoming totally surf-stoked. Once you experience this phenomenon, you can lose connection with anything and everything except your peers down on the beach, and the values the waves and ocean force upon you, whether you like it or not."

In the eye of the storm and not a hair out of place: former world champ Derek Ho streaking through the tunnel at the Pipeline.

INSET: Buttons Kaluhiokalani flashes the peace sign on the way out, c. 1975.

Strapsurfing

Strapsurfing (or tow-in surfing) is the sport's most recent leading edge. There were the 10-second noserides of David Nuuhiwa back in the '60s; the five-second tube rides of Shaun Tomson and Rabbit, of Davey Miller and Lopez in the '70s; the 25-foot waves of Waimea, Makaha and Third Reef Pipeline ridden by Greg Noll, George Downing, Pat Curren, Reno Abellira, Owl Chapman, Mark Richards, Keone Downing, Ken Bradshaw, Brock Little, Derrick Doernerand and a bunch of other guys over the last 40 years. But somewhere around 25 feet seems to be the limit for what an unassisted individual can ride. It has to do with the speed of the wave, the speed a man can paddle, the speed of the wind and water moving up the face of the wave, and how fast gravity (working with all that friction) can pull a surfer toward the bottom of the wave and into the business section.

But if you *pull* a guy into such an impossible wave using a boat of some kind, or one of those Jet Ski–type things, you've got the boardspeed to pick up the wave a lot sooner, when it's still building toward vertical. With JATO (jet-assisted take-off), you're stylin', if you don't make a mistake, or if you don't push it too far — taking off too deep or too late or on a wave that can't be made. And because your feet are tucked securely into footstraps on your surfboard, the moguls of chop that would normally lead to a sure wipeout are ramps to blast over, the way windsurfers do.

As it turned out, it was the windsurfers who started strapsurfing. Laird Hamilton and Buzzy Kerbox and big-wave surfer Derrick Doerner began using an inflatable Zodiac to tow each other into outer-reef waves off the North Shore, where only extraordinary windsurfers like Robby Naish had ridden the waves before. Being powered into a wave by a sail was like being towed in, but if you were towed in, you didn't have to contend with the sail once you were surfing! Over on Maui, windsurfers Mike Waltze, David Kalama, Rush Randle, Josh and Mark Angulo and Peter Cabrinha were beginning to sail a big-wave spot called Jaws. Hamilton and Kerbox became aware of what the Maui windsurfers were doing about the time Bruce Brown and his *Endless Summer II* crew were in the islands hoping to do an outer-reef segment for the film. So it all came together: surfboards, surfers, outer reefs, windsurfers, straps, WaveRunners, cameras and giant waves. Jaws became a kind of millennial Waimea, and images of surfers on 40-foot waves — so recently an impossibility and always hair-raising — became almost commonplace.

shaping, glassing, the works) – Bump boards, reproductions, everything – for the Japanese market and for private collectors: from the shaping room to the collector's shelf!

Greg Noll, who sold 50 old boards for 50 bucks apiece when he moved north to Crescent City, California, says he could get at least a couple thousand each now. A commercial fisherman, he's been shaping a few *olo* reproductions for special customers. "The first was red cedar; in three days of working it down, I burnt the armature out of my Porter Cable power planer, one of the toughest on the market, and it still took six kids to get it on the car and home to finish. It was the same dimensions as a koa wood *olo* found on Kaua'i in a burial cave, and the Hawai'ians had to go up into the hills, fell it with a stone adze, smooth it with sand and get it down to water from the mountains – without wheels!" Yes, respect for the old ways is being revived.

Today, there are surf magazines in Japan, England, Ireland, South Africa, France, Spain, Canada, Brazil and probably a few other countries. There are dozens of surf-hotlines, on the phone and on the Net, that provide up-to-the-minute wave conditions at any spot you may want to surf, taking plenty of the guesswork (and arguably some of the mystery and adventure) out of the search. Surfline, for instance, offers spot checks up and down the coasts of the United States and Hawai'i; several of the sites are equipped with video cameras that send photographs of the waves and conditions, updated every minute. There are also links to WaveTrak International, which creates live connections to surf reports around the world, including virtual real-time looks at some famous spots, like Biarritz in France and the Narrabeen-Collaroy beach or the Gold Coast in Australia. Even surfing music has come back big-time, even though most of the bands playing it have never been near an ocean, the Butt-Hole Surfers excepted.

Each generation pushes the performance envelope farther into the impossible realms. A great windsurfer, Laird Hamilton was one of the first to experiment with strapsurfing. Here he fires off a corkscrew 360 at Off the Wall, a move his father, Bill, would never have imagined.

FOLLOWING SPREAD: Windsurfers pioneered the outer reef waves of Hawai'i, and the surfers followed. Windsurfing's great Robby Naish at Jaws.

It is ironic to some that Nat Young, who sounded the death knell of the noseriding era and spearheaded the shortboard revolution, should have been a central inspiration in the creation of the ASP's World Professional Longboard Championship. But it's true. Nat exemplifies the surfer as waterman, with a wide range of skills and the ability to use the appropriate vehicle for the conditions. And sometimes that means a big surfboard!

Snowboarding, skateboarding, windsurfing, kite surfing, strapsurfing, wakeboarding, skysurfing and other spinoff board sports and related cultural styles have their roots in the sport of Hawai'ian kings. There are professional and amateur surfers who compete at surf spots all around the world, yet the vast majority of surfers never compete. Instead they seek out solitude and bear the discomforts that go with it – the frigid waters of the Oregon shore, the harsh desert remoteness of the Namibia coast, the life-threatening waves of Hawai'i's outer reefs. There are millions of kids out there on their Boogie Boards, assimilating the wisdom of wave motion and absorbing the sheer magnificence and beauty of the spinning waves, playing in nature's most brilliant playground.

Apartheid has been abolished in South Africa, and surfers are once again trekking out to Jeffrey's Bay, perhaps the world's finest "right-hander." There are surf museums celebrating the history of the sport, there are art galleries and shows devoted to its art and artifacts, there are restaurants celebrating its theme, there are woody clubs and woody rallies celebrating the classic surf car. There are craftsmen (like Pat Curren and Malcolm Wilson) making miniature reproductions of classic surfboards and even classic beach dioramas. There is a Watermen's Ball and an annual Surf Legends get-together (held at a different fabulous surfing beach each year).

The thruster may be here to stay, but the longboard is back. "Today, 65 years later, many surfers are rediscovering their heritage just as Duke did," wrote soul surfer David Parmenter. "The biggest trend in surfing today is a worldwide shift to the longboard. You can scream and rant and bang your head on the floor, you can scrawl hate with wax on the sidewalk, you can send seething letters to the editor about fat old kooks on logs…but it won't change the evident fact that, demographically, longboarding is modern surfing. Or more exactly, postmodern surfing." ["Epoch-alypse Now: Postmodern Surfing in the Age of Reason," *The Surfer's Journal*, Vol. 4, No. 4]

In 1997, Wally Froiseth, still "surf drunk" in his seventies, said he reckons the appeal of surfing is being in nature and, of course, the challenge – and *standing up*: "My folks used to tell me, don't stand up, it's too dangerous." How right they were. Wally was a key man in designing the *Hawai'iloa*, the 62-foot Polynesian voyaging canoe built from logs donated by the Tlingit, Haida and Tsimshian tribes of Southeast Alaska. The 200-foot-tall trees were seven feet in diameter and more than 400 years old. "They were spruce, cut off at the top," says Froiseth. "They shaped 'em out and made 'em into sailing canoes. They sailed to Tahiti, the Marquesas, then they shipped 'em up to Seattle, and we went up there to show 'em the results, and they were really happy. They treated us like kings." Froiseth had the honor of captaining *Hawai'iloa* on the last leg of her journey from Ketchikan to Juneau in 1995. Froiseth and George Downing have every important board they ever made and surfed safely stashed away.

Surf nostalgia is big business in the latter days of the millennium. Good-time "legends" events function somewhat like senior golf tournaments, getting old stars together to share a few waves, luaus and stories. You can slice the charisma with a knife!

ABOVE: **Tom and Pat Curren span a period of unprecedented change in the sport.**

In modest-sized waves, surfing can be more fun than threatening. Sometimes there's plenty of time to just enjoy it all.

ABOVE: **Six-year-old Timothy James drops in at Velzyland.**

OPPOSITE, TOP: **Victor Lopez sets up an evening barrel ride at the Pipeline (see following pages).**

OPPOSITE, BOTTOM: **Underwater tri-fin, winter '92–'93, North Shore.**

THE STOKE

At its best, surfing remains play – easy play or big serious play – and that is the meaning that this unshakable word – *stoked!* – keeps before us. *Sport* is way too mindless a word for what surfing is, and art is way too complimentary to the vast majority of surfers. *Martial art* might locate it best in the body-mind continuum, since surfing offers many of the self-development qualities sought by seekers of one kind or another. Yes, surfing is like aikido, using the power of the wave to the surfer's own advantage. But a surfer is a different sort of creature, too, a natural athlete who lives much of his or her life outside the ordinary boundaries of society and civilization, addicted to the juice inherent in the wave-riding experience.

The beach is a no-man's-land and a borderland, a desert and a wasteland. Not only the meeting of land and sea, it's the place where law and order meet divinely organized chaos. Surf culture is anarchic, but it has its own code. "To live outside the law you must be honest," sang Bob Dylan, and nature does have a way of keeping you honest … and persistent.

Like Northern California surfer Dale Webster, who's taken on the personal goal of surfing an entire lunar year – three good rides a day for 28 years, more than 10,000 days in a row! Inspired by his friend, the late Rick Griffin, he is relentless. Meanwhile, he and another friend have launched Project 7, a full-bore attempt to restore the integrity of the Russian River watershed and consequently the beach and offshore environment where he surfs. Politicians in Sacramento see these guys as crackpots, but they persist. That's what surfers are trained to do. Especially when there are waves at stake.

Although the public image of a surfer is often that of a "duh"-speaking knuckle-dragger, some of the most eloquent and sophisticated people in the world are surfers. Midget Farrelly is a good example. Asked, "What is your goal in surfing?" in an interview in 1968, Midget's response was, in part: "The genuine surfer cannot afford too much fame. The genuine surfer can-

The Pipeline is the archetype of the perfect surfer's wave, so ideal at times that it almost mocks reality. How could something as transient and ineffable as a wave continue to articulate such a specific natural syllable so precisely over so many years? How, year after year, do infinite variables combine to yield these recurring perfect chords?

not afford to be isolated in his own break. The genuine surfer cannot afford to look after a million dollars. The genuine surfer cannot afford to dominate competition. He becomes an unfortunate pathetic object of people's attentions when he does. The surfer must be pure, hard, calculating, precise. He must be a combination of a spartan athlete, a technologist, a futuristic spaceman of the waves. Not so much an image hero, millionaire, champion and success. This is the psychology he must take on if he is to truly succeed within himself in surfing."

It's like Dr. Timothy Leary said: "It's perfectly logical to me that surfing is the spiritual aesthetic style of the liberated self. And that's the model for the future." [*Surfer*, January 1978] The stoke of surfing is one of those wordless conditions that you have to experience to know – wordless but powerful, since it is the invisible center around which all surf culture orbits.

Surfing is magic –
riding echoes of cosmic energy, transmitted through vast tracks
of ocean, at the wild fringes of continents.

Acknowledgements & Thanks

To Steve Pezman, who has greased the wheels of our surfers' universe and keeps us all connecting and connecting and connecting.

To Craig Stecyk, who downloaded his immense understanding of several areas in a most inspiring way.

To Art Brewer, who beat the bushes and shook the trees in search of gems from the finest photographers of surf and surf culture.

To Lori Rick, who picked up my 100,000-word manuscript, said there was room for half of it, then skillfully guided the streamlining process.

For their gracious assistance: Robert Avellan, Dr. John Ball, Bruce Brown, James Cassimus, Jeff Divine, George Downing, Pierce Flynn, Wally Froiseth, Leroy Grannis, Glenn Hening, Kit Horn, Archie Kalepa, Don Kremers, Gary Lynch, Charlie Lyon, Greg MacGillivray, Alain Mazer, Greg Noll, Craig Peterson, Joe Quigg, John Severson, Allan Seymour, Dale Velzy, Matt Warshaw, Jeff Werve, Jeremy Xavier, Reynolds Yater, Nat Young.

And to my wife Susan, best of all possible friends, my son Alex, best of all possible sons, and my daughter Alana, best of all possible horse-loving daughters.

BIBLIOGRAPHY

Alpers, Antony. *Legends of the South Seas.* New York: T.Y. Crowell, 1970.

Babitz, Eve. "Surf's Up: The Artist Outlaw Who Turns Rainbow Fades into Lucky $135 Stars." *Rolling Stone* (June 20, 1974).

Bascom, Willard. *Waves and Beaches: The Dynamics of the Ocean Surface.* Garden City, NY: Doubleday Anchor, 1964.

Beaglehole, John C., ed. "The Voyage of the Resolution and Discovery," *Journal of Captain James Cook,* Cambridge, MA: University Press, 1967.

Bingham, Hiram. *A Residence of Twenty-one Years in the Sandwich Islands.* New York: Converse, 1847.

Bird, Isabella L. *The Hawaiian Archipelago: Six Months Amongst the Palm Groves, Coral Reefs, and Volcanos of the Sandwich Islands.* London: John Murray, 1876.

Blair, John. *The Illustrated Discography of Surf Music, 1959–1965.* Riverside, California: J. Bee Productions, 1978.

Blake, Tom. *Hawaiian Surfboard,* Paradise of the Pacific Press: Honolulu, 1935. Carroll, Nick, ed. The Next Wave. New York: Abbeville Press, 1991.

Crawford, Carin. "Waves of Transformation." Internet essay (June 1993).

Daws, Gavan. *Shoal of Time: A History of the Hawaiian Islands.* New York: Macmillan, 1968.

Duane, Daniel. *Caught Inside: A Surfer's Year on the California Coast.* New York: North Point Press, 1996.

Edwards, Phil, with Bob Ottum. *You Should Have Been Here an Hour Ago.* New York: Harper & Row, 1967.

Farrelly, Midget, with Craig McGregor. *The Surfing Life.* New York: Arco, 1967.

Finney, Ben, & James D, Houston. *Surfing: A History of the Ancient Hawaiian Sport.* San Francisco: Pomegranate Artbooks, 1996.

Gross, M. Grant. *Oceanography: A View of the Earth.* Englewood Cliffs, NJ: Prentice-Hall, 1972.

Henning, Glenn and Maureen. *Groundswell Society Annual Publication. First Edition.* Oxnard Shores, California: 1997.

Jarratt, Phil. *Mr Sunset: The Jeff Hakman Story.* London: Gen X Publishing, 1997. Los Angeles: General Publishing Group, 1997.

Jarves, James J. *History of the Hawaiian or Sandwich Islands.* London: Edward Moxon, 1843.

Kampion, Drew. *The Book of Waves.* Santa Barbara: Arpel/Surfer, 1989.

Kelly, Jr., John. *Surf and Sea.* New York: A.S. Barnes, 1965.

Kinsman, Blair. *Wind Waves: Their Generation and Propagation on the Ocean Surface.* Englewood Cliffs: Prentice-Hall, NJ, 1965.

Klein, H. Arthur. *Surfing.* Philadelphia & New York: Lippincott, 1965.

Knox, David. *Mark Richards: A Surfing Legend.* Australia: Angus & Robertson, 1992.

London, Jack. *Cruise of the Snark.* New York: MacMillan, 1911.

Lueras, Leonard. *Surfing: The Ultimate Pleasure.* New York: Workman Publishing, 1984.

Margan, Frank, and Ben Finney. *A Pictorial History of Surfing.* Sydney, Australia: Paul Hamlyn, 1970.

Michener, James A. *Hawaii.* New York: Random House, 1959.

Nadeau, Remi. *California: The New Society.* New York: David McKay Co., 1963.

Noll, Greg, and Andrea Gabbard. *Da Bull: Life over the Edge.* Bozeman, Montana: Bangtail Press, 1989.

Pearson, Kent. *Surfing Subcultures of Australia and New Zealand.* St. Lucia, Qld.: Univ. of Queensland Press, 1979.

Pukui, Mary Kawena, and Samuel H. Elbert. *Hawaiian Dictionary.* Honolulu: University Press of Hawaii, 1971.

Severson, John. *Modern Surfing around the World.* New York: Doubleday, 1964.

–, ed. *Great Surfing.* New York: Doubleday, 1967

Steele, H. Thomas. *The Hawaiian Shirt.* New York: Abbeville Press, 1984.

Stern, David H., and William S. Cleary. *Surfing Guide to Southern California.* Malibu: The Fitzpatrick Co., 1963.

Thrum, Thomas G. *Hawaiian Folk Tales.* Chicago: A.C. McClurg, 1921.

– *More Hawaiian Folk Tales.* Chicago: A.C. McClurg, 1923.

Toffler, Alvin. *Future Shock.* New York: Random House, 1970.

Twain, Mark. *Mark Twain's Letters from Hawaii.* New York: Appleton-Century, 1966.

– *Mark Twain's West.* Chicago: R.R. Donnelley, 1983.

– *Roughing It.* Hartford, Connecticut: American Publishing Co., 1872

Van Dyke, Fred. *30 Years of Riding the World's Biggest Waves.* Santa Cruz: Ocean Sports International, 1988.

Warshaw, Matt. *Surfriders.* Del Mar, California: Tehabi Books, 1997.

Wolfe, Tom. *The Pump House Gang.* New York: Farrar, Straus & Giroux, 1968.

Young, Nat. *The History of Surfing* (Revised Edition). Angourie (NSW, Australia): Palm Beach Press, 1983 and '94.

– *Surfing Fundamentals.* Los Angeles: The Body Press, 1985.

* Note: The definitions cited in this book are from The Random House Dictionary of the English Language (New York: Random House, 1967), a single heavy volume, which I received from John Severson on my birthday in 1969, when I was editor of *Surfer.*

* Another Note: Uncredited interviews were conducted by the author.

PHOTO CREDITS

Page

1: UFOs/Mike Moir

2–3: Herbie Fletcher at Maalaea/Art Brewer

4–5: Surfers at Sunset/Steve Sakamoto

6–7: Serious energy at Mavericks/Bob Barbour

8–9: Pipeline/Rick Doyle

10–11: Surf now!/Brian Sprout

13: Troy Teck/Newport Beach/Mike Moir

14–15: Makaha crew, c. 1950/Joe Quigg

17: "North Shore Combo Plate" (1988) John Severson

21: Bruce Brown/Courtesy Bruce Brown Films

22: Sunset Beach swells/Drew Kampion

23: Drew Kampion, Puerto Rico/LeRoy Grannis

24: Pipeline/Art Brewer

25: Drew Kampion, 1969/John Severson

26–27: Burleigh Head, Australia/Lee Pegus

27: Kevin Naughton/Fiji Craig Peterson

28: Petroglyph/Drew Kampion Collection

29: Surfer at Waikiki, 1890s/Courtesy Bishop Museum

30: Maids on a Wave/Wallace Mackay, from *Summer Cruising in the South Seas*, 1874/Courtesy Bishop Museum

31: Kraimoku Homestead by Villroy, 1825/Courtesy Bishop Museum

32: Cook at Kealakekua Bay/Courtesy Bishop Museum

33: "Homage to Capt. Cook"/C.R. Stecyk III

34–35: Waikiki, c. 1910 Alonzo Gartley/Courtesy Bishop Museum

34: Jack & Charmian London, 1915/Courtesy Bishop Museum

34: "Trip to Hawaii" cover/DeSoto Brown Collection

34: "Honolulu" cover/DeSoto Brown Collection

36–37: Waikiki & Outrigger Club, 1908/Courtesy Bishop Museum

36: Three Hawai'ian Princes/Courtesy Bishop Museum

37: George Freeth at Redondo, 1907/Courtesy Dr. John Ball

38: 1914 Mid-Pacific Surf Carnival poster/Courtesy Bishop Museum

38: Waikiki beach boys, c. 1925/Courtesy Bishop Museum

38: Surfboarders at Waikiki, c. 1915/Courtesy Bishop Museum

39: Catching a wave near Diamond Head, 1925 *Honolulu Advertiser*/Courtesy Bishop Museum

40: Duke Kahanamoku at Freshwater, Australia/Courtesy Bishop Museum

40: Duke's board en route to Freshwater/Courtesy Bishop Museum

40: (background) Duke and spectators at Freshwater/Courtesy Bishop Museum

41: Waikiki surf antics/DeSoto Brown Collection

41: scene from *Two Dukes in The Wake of the Red Witch*/Courtesy Surfer magazine

42–43: "Jeux Haviens"/Courtesy Bishop Museum

43: Tom Morey in Bali/Jim Russi

44: Tom Blake with board collection, 1930/Courtesy Bishop Museum

44: Tom Blake hollow board logo, 1940/Hawaiian Historical Society

45: Tom Blake & Duke Kahanamoku, c. 1935/ Courtesy Surfer magazine

46–47: Paddlers at San Onofre surf contest, 1940/ Dr. John Ball

48: San Onofre, 1939/Doc Ball, Courtesy Jack Reinhold

49: California '30s boards/Courtesy Sam Ryan Collection

49: Paddleboard vs. plank at Paddleboard Cove/ Dr. Don James, Craig Stecyk Collection

49: Hermosa Beach and PV guys at Curries, 1946/ LeRoy Grannis

50–51: Surfing at Paddleboard Cove, 1935/ Dr. John Ball

52: San Onofre jam session, 1947/Joe Quigg

53: Malibu 1950/Joe Quigg

54: Hot Curl board/Craig Stecyk Collection

54: Blackie Makaena at Canoes, 1950/Bud Browne

54: Makaha Hot Curl crew, c. 1950/Wally Froiseth Collection

55: Norma Jean Baker, Pete Peterson & Tom Zahn/Courtesy Surfer magazine

55: Malibu grouping, summer of '51/Joe Quigg

56: Simmons' car & board/Joe Quigg/ Courtesy Reynolds Yater

56: Joe Quigg, Matt Kivlin & Tom Zahn, c. 1949/ Joe Quigg

56–57: (background) Bob Simmons holds forth on hydrodynamics Joe Quigg/ Courtesy Reynolds Yater

57: Dave Syre & Peter Cole at Malibu, 1949/Joe Quigg

57: Shaping balsa in Velzy's garage, 1950/Dale Velzy, Craig Stecyk Collection

58–59: Tom Zahn at Malibu, 1952/Joe Quigg

60: Makaha shack interior, c. 1950/Courtesy Walter Hoffman

60: Makaha shack, c. 1950/Courtesy Walter Hoffman

60: Makaha crew, c. 1950/Courtesy Walter Hoffman

61: The Calhouns at Makaha, 1962/LeRoy Grannis

61: Walter Hoffman & surf car, c. 1950/ Courtesy Walter Hoffman

62–63: Waimea Bay, November 7, 1957 Dr. Don James/Courtesy Walter Hoffman

63: First day Waimea crew/Courtesy Mickey Muñoz

64: Bud Browne at Makaha, 1962/LeRoy Grannis

64: Poster for *Cat on a Hot Foam Board*/Courtesy Bud Browne

65: Dr. Don James at Makaha, 1962/Leroy Grannis

65: Dr. James Ball, Paddleboard Cove, c. 1938/Tom Blake

66: Santa Cruz Surfing Club, 1940/LeRoy Grannis

66–67: Australian Surf Cars, c. 1958/Courtesy Surfer magazine

67: US Team to Surf Carnival, 1956/Greg Noll Collection

68: Greg Noll Surf Shop, Hermosa Beach, 1964/ LeRoy Grannis

68: Jacobs Surf Shop, Hermosa Beach, 1964/ LeRoy Grannis

68: Velzy Surfboards logo/Tom Servais

69: Hobie Alter & Phil Edwards, c. 1964/Courtesy Surfer magazine

69: Hobie surfboards logo/Courtesy Surfer magazine

69: (background) Foam blanks at Clark Foam/ Jeff Divine

70–71: Wave at Ha'apiti, Moorea/Art Brewer

71: Rincon Point, 1947/Joe Quigg

72: Texas Beach, c. 1964/Ron Stoner

73: Greg Noll factory party, 1965/LeRoy Grannis

74: Gidget at Malibu, mid-'50s/Kathy Kohner Collection

75: *Muscle Beach* Party poster/American International Pictures

75: Kathy Kohner & Sandra Dee on set of *Gidget*/Kathy Kohner Collection

75: Gidget book cover/Kathy Kohner Collection

76: *Surfin' Safari* album/Capitol Records

76: Bondi stompers, c. 1965/Ron Perrott

77: Dick Dale with His Del-Tones, 1963/Courtesy Michael Ochs Archives

77: *Surfers' Choice* album, 1961/Collection of Don Kremers

78: Fender guitar ad, John Martin, 1965/Bob Perine, Courtesy Fender Musical Collections from the Stephen K. Peeples Archives

79: Ralph's Beach Boys/Craig Stecyk Collection

79: Jan & Dean/Courtesy Michael Ochs Archives

80–81: Malibu Surfrider Beach, summer '62/ LeRoy Grannis

82: Surf Nazi/William Cleary

83: Lance Carson at Malibu, 1962/LeRoy Grannis

84: Mickey Dora at Malibu, c. 1960/Kathy Kohner Collection

84: Mickey Dora surfing in France, 1972/Hal Jepsen Films, Courtesy Surfer magazine

84–85: (background) Mickey Dora in top hat, 1969/Craig Stecyk

85: Mickey Dora & Malibu victim (sequence)/Brad Barrett/Surfer magazine

86–87: Mickey Dora at Malibu, '65/Ron Stoner/Surfer magazine

88: Postering for *Free and Easy*/MacGillivray-Freeman Films

88: John Severson in 1959/Louise Severson

89: *Going My Wave* poster/John Severson

89: *Barefoot Adventure* poster/Bruce Brown Films

89: *Outside the Third Dimension* poster/MacGillivray-Freeman Films

89: (background) The Bay Theater, 1975/Greg MacGillivray

90–91: John Severson at Trestles, Oct. '65/Ron Stoner/Surfer magazine

91: Corky Carroll & Sherri Haley in Keds ad/Courtesy Surfer magazine

91: Calhoun skaters in Laguna, '67/LeRoy Grannis

92: The first Surfer/Courtesy Surfer Publications

93: *International Surfing*, Sept. 1967/Courtesy Surfing magazine/Western Empire Publications

93: Australian Tracks/Courtesy Surfer magazine

93: Surfer reader in Africa, 1972/Craig Peterson

94–95: Phil Edwards, Banzai Pipeline, 1963/Dr. Don James

96: Formal O'Neill wetsuits, Africa, c. 1975/ Dan Merkle/Courtesy O'Neill, Inc.

97: Larry Bertlemann Katin ad/Art Brewer

97: 7Up ad, c. 1960/Allan Seymour Collection

97: Hang-Ten ad, 1964/Courtesy *Surfer* magazine
98: Greg Noll at Pipeline, c. 1965/John Severson
99: Jock Sutherland at Pipeline, c. 1965/LeRoy Grannis
99: Gary Propper & Claude Codgen/Richard Graham
100–101: "The Beast" at Velzyland, c. 1962/ Leo Hetzel
101: David Nuuhiwa, '72 World Contest/Drew Kampion
102: Joey Cabell vs. el toro, Peru '65/Leo Hetzel
103: Tom Morey Invitational poster/Steve Wilkings Collection
103: Pat & Tom Curren, early '60s/Leo Hetzel
104: David Nuuhiwa on the nose, Malibu '67/Steve Wilkings
105: Corky Carroll at Poche, July '65/Ron Stoner/ Surfer magazine
106: Bob McTavish, Long Reef, '67/John Witzig
106: Midget Farrelly, Long Reef, '61/Ron Perrott
107: Nat Young with trophy, San Diego '66/Ron Stoner/*Surfer* magazine
107: Nat Young, Honolua Bay '67/John Witzig
108: Bob McTavish/Richard Graham
108: George Greenough/John Witzig
109: *Endless Summer* poster/Bruce Brown Films
109: *Endless Summer* crew in Africa/Bruce Brown Films
109: (background) Bruce with camera/Bruce Brown Films
110: Duke Kahanamoku, San Diego '66/Ron *Stoner*/Surfer magazine
110: Nat Young, Australia, 1967/Alby Falzon
111: Dick Brewer, 1968/David Darling
112: George Greenough at Lennox Head, '67/John Witzig
112: Bill Barnfield/Jeff Divine
113: Dewey Weber/Richard Graham
113: *Five Summer* Stories Poster/MacGillivray-Freeman Films
113: Dewey Weber Surfboard Logo/Jim Russi
114: Corky Carroll Jantzen Ad/Courtesy Jantzen Sportswear
115: Rick Griffin at the Ranch, 1969/Drew Kampion
115: Murphy Surfer, 1962/Rick Griffin/Surfer magazine
116: Bunker Spreckels, Backdoor Pipeline '69/Peter French
116: Bunker Spreckels with red board, 1969/ Art Brewer
117: Dale Velzy, Jack's Surfboards ad, 1969/Don Kremers/Courtesy *Surfer* magazine
117: Challenger Surfboards ad, 1969/Don Kremers/ Courtesy *Surfer* magazine
118: Nat Young at Haleiwa, Dec. '68/Ron Stoner
119: Owl Chapman at Maalaea, 1976/Steve Wilkings
119: Barry Kanaiaupuni at Honolua Bay, 1972/Art Brewer
120: Marine confiscation at Trestles, '69/Ron Stoner
120: Johanna roadsign, 1970/Drew Kampion
120: (background) West African wreck/Craig Peterson
121: Johanna pasture parking, 1970/Drew Kampion
121: Rolf Aurness at Malibu AAAA contest, 1969/ Brad Barrett/*Surfer* magazine
122–123: Honolua Bay/Jim Cassimus
123: Surfers & Dolphin/Rick Doyle
124: Flyaway cutout with leash/Steve Wilkings

125: Surfing Again! tee shirt/Mike Moir
126: Lunada Bay trail/Jim Russi
126: Morocco, January '75/Craig Peterson
127: Mike Stewart, North Shore, '92/Rick Doyle
128: Gary Elkerton at G-Land/Jeff Divine
128: Steve Pezman with Dr. Timothy Leary/Art Brewer
129: Morocco, '84/Darrell Jones
129: Rick Griffin drives MotorSkill/Art Brewer
129: Rolling in Mexico, 1976/Tim Bernardy
130–131: Glen Campbell in New Zealand/Mike Moir
132: North Shore line-up, c. 1975/Nat Young Collection
133: Rick Rasmussen, Long Island, 1977/Drew Kampion
133: Jeff Hakman at Off The Wall, North Shore, 1971/Steve Wilkings
134–135: Gerry Lopez at Pipeline (sequence), 1975/Steve Wilkings
134–135: Gerry Lopez at Pipeline/Jeff Divine
136: Eddie Aikau at Waimea Bay, 1978/ Steve Wilkings
136: Hawai'i's Aikau family/Steve Wilkings
137: Eddie Aikau Memorial, Waimea Bay, 1978/ Steve Wilkings
138–139: Oceanside contest from the pier/Mike Moir
140: Huntington Beach Riot, 1986/Aaron Chang
141: Scene from *Big Wednesday* Warner Bros./ Courtesy *Surfer* magazine
141: *Big Wednesday* poster/John Severson
141: Scene from *Apocalypse Now*/Zoetrope Studios/Courtesy *Surfer* magazine
141: *Free Ride* poster/Bill Delany Films
142: Newport Wedge colors, '88/Mike Moir
142: Haleiwa Surf Shop/Rick Doyle
143: Simon Anderson with Thruster/Peter Crawford
143: Richard Schmidt, North Shore quiver/James Cassimus
144: Bronzed Aussies/Collection of Drew Kampion
144: Caution Sign/Jeff Divine
145: No Surfing Contests/Jeff Divine
145: Lord Blears & Mark Richards/James Cassimus
146–147: Sonny Garcia at US Open/Jeff Divine
147: Tom Carroll celebrates/Jim Russi
147: English surf signage 1976/Jeff Divine
148–149: Gerry Lopez at Pipeline/James Cassimus
149: Matt Patterson, Huntington Beach/Mike Moir
150: Tom Carroll, '91 Pipeline Masters/Art Brewer
151: Tom Curren, Off the Wall, 1987/Jim Russi
152: Malia Jones, 1996/Jeff Divine
153: Margo Godfrey at Hammonds Reef, 1967/Ron Stoner/*Surfer* magazine
153: Margo Godfrey Oberg, Kauai, 1977/Jeff Divine
154: Lisa Andersen triptych/Art Brewer
154–155: Lisa Andersen surfing/Art Brewer
156: Kelly Slater with Bob McKnight/Jim Russi
156: Kelly Slater at Waimea Bay/Jim Russi
157: Eddie Vedder & Pierce Flynn/Courtesy Surfrider Foundation
157: MOM album/Courtesy Surfrider Foundation
157: Baja surf camp, c. 1987/Art Brewer
158–159: Surfrider protest paddle in France/ Art Brewer
161: Newport Wedge colors, 1987/Mike Moir

161: Einstein imagination/Rick Rietveld
161: Mickey Muñoz sandals/Art Brewer
162: Wilbur Kookmeyer, July '89/Bob Penuelas/*Surfer* magazine
162: Newport kids, c. 1987/Mike Moir
163: Coco Harrison/Art Brewer
163: Classic woody/Ron Stoner/*Surfer* magazine
164: Corky Carroll: A Surfer for President/Art Brewer
164: Gerry Lopez: Chairman of the Board/Art Brewer
164–165: Mark Richards at Pipeline, c. late '70s/Rick Doyle
166: Christian Fletcher at Trestles, '89/Jeff Divine
167: Santa Cruz contest crowd/Drew Kampion
167: *Beach Culture* magazine/Surfer Publications
168: Locals Only/Jeff Divine
168: The Fletcher family/Art Brewer
169: Crowded lineup/Rick Doyle
170–171: Five young grommets/Jim Russi
172–173: Bailing at the Pipeline/Brian Bielmann
173: Frog House shark art/Mike Moir
174: Kelly Slater & fans/Jim Russi
175: Mark Cunningham underwater/Art Brewer
176: Strap surfers on Maui/Erik Aeder
177: Web Surfer/College Shopping Network
177: Kelly Slater cover, May 1996/Courtesy *Interview magazine*
178–179: Mark Foo at Mavericks (sequence)/Robert Brown
178: Donnie Solomon at Waimea/Bernie Baker
179: Alec Cooke rescue/Darrell Jones
180: Derek Doerner at Waimea/Jim Russi
181: Laird Hamilton & David Kalama at Jaws/Erik Aeder
182–183: Laird Hamilton at Jaws, 1995/Erik Aeder
184: John Caster shaping/Mike Moir
184: "Discovery" (1978)/John Severson
185: "Trestles" (1993)/Ken Auster
185–186: Sequence Surfing Sketch (1997)/Russell Crotty
186: "Surf City Here We Come" (1979)/Lynn Coleman
187: "Stoked!" (1997)/Steve Valiere
188: The Surfer's Journal, vol. 3, no. 2
188: *Wahini* magazine, vol. 3, no. 2
188: G-Land accommodations/Jeff Divine
189: Wavepool, Allentown, Pennsylvania/Rick Doyle
190–191: Derek Ho at Pipeline, 1989/Jim Russi
191: Buttons Kaluhiokalani, c. 1975/Jeff Divine
192–193: Laird Hamilton corkscrew (sequence)/Art Brewer
192–193: (background) Tow-in/Erik Aeder
194–195: Robby Naish at Jaws, Maui, 1996/Erik Aeder
196: Nat Young, 1993/Jim Russi
197: Surf Legends at Makaha, 1993/Bernie Baker
197: San Onofre Classic poster/Allan Seymour Collection
197: Tom & Pat Curren, 1995/Mike Moir
198: "TJ" at Velzyland/Rob Gilley
199: Victor Lopez at Pipeline/Art Brewer
199: Underwater Thruster/Rick Doyle
200: Victor Lopez at Pipeline (sequence)/Art Brewer
202–203: Rock Dancers at Steamer Lane, 1989/Rick Doyle
204–205: Inside Sunset/Art Brewer
206–207: Waimea dress circle/Rob Gilley
208–209: Evening on the North Shore/Peter French

INDEX

A

Aaberg, Denny, 140
advertising, 91, 92, 96–97, 111, 114, 115, 125, 161, 162, 164
Aikau, Eddie, 136, 137
alaia, 30
Allen, Paul, 109
Alter, Hobie, 21, 68, 69, 73, 94, 97
Andersen, Lisa, 153, 154, 155
Anderson, Simon, 143, 144
art, kinetic, surfing as, 149
art, surf, 184, 186, 188, 197
Association of Surfing Professionals, 153
auctions, surfboard, 189
August, Robert, 24, 109
Aurness, Rolf, 117, 120, 121, 150
Auster, Ken, 184, 185
Australian surfing, 27, 40, 66–68, 104–107, 112, 113, 121, 123, 136 137, 143, 144, 151, 153, 157

B

Bagley, Bob, 92
Bali, 123, 132, 133
Ball, Dr. John, 50, 65
balsa chip boards, 56–57, 68, 69
Bartholomew, Wayne, 136
Baywatch (television show), 156, 175
"beachboy" concept, 38, 40
Beach Boys, 76, 77, 79
beach culture, 175
Beach Culture (magazine), 163, 167
bibliography, 211
big-wave surf subculture, 61, 63, 66–67, 99, 129, 136–137, 151, 177, 178, 180
Big Wednesday (film), 137, 140, 141, 142
Billabong sportswear, 161, 162, 163, 170
Bing Surfboards, 111
Blair, John, 76
Blake, Tom, 44, 45, 48, 50, 56, 65
Blum, Eric, 108
bodysurfing, 127, 175
Boogie Board, 104, 127, 196
books, on surfing, 92–93, 176, 188
Botha, Wendy, 154
Boyer, Lynn, 153
Brewer, Dick, 111
Brown, Bruce, 21, 88, 92, 94, 104, 109, 125, 168, 192
Brown, Woody, 59, 60
Browne, Bud, 61, 64–65, 89, 140
Burnside, Bob, 68

C

Cabell, Joey, 103, 106, 164
Cairns, Ian, 136, 140, 144, 151, 153
Calhoun, Candy, 61, 91, 92
Calhoun, Marge, 61, 91, 92, 153
Calhoun, Robyn, 61, 91, 92
California surfing, 120, 138–139, 140, 156–157, 158–159. See also Malibu, California; San Onofre, California and
beach films, 69, 73–76, 85
"hot dog" style, 57, 82, 84
and surf music, 76–79
camps. See surf camps
Carroll, Corky, 73, 91, 92, 97, 103, 104, 105, 113, 114, 115, 120, 144, 164
Carroll, Tom, 146, 150, 151
cars, surf, 66–67, 100–101, 163
Carson, Lance, 24, 82, 83, 158
Casper, John, 184
Cerney, Walt, 168, 170–171
Chapman, Owl, 119
Chesser, Todd, 178–180
Church, Harry, 66
Clark, Gordon, 21, 69, 157
Clark, Jeff, 177–178
clothing, surf-based, 61, 82, 96, 97, 125, 133, 138–139, 140, 142, 160–162
Codgen, Claude, 98
Cole, Peter, 61, 65, 103
Coleman, Lynn, 186
competitive paddling, 44, 144
competitive surfing, 60, 103–104, 106–107, 113, 125, 132, 137, 144–146, 167, 196
apathy toward, 113, 117, 150
Cook, James, 30, 32, 33, 65
Cross, Dickie, 59, 60, 63
Crotty, Russell, 185–186
Cunningham, Mark, 175
Curren, Pat, 97, 103, 197
Curren, Tom, 103, 151, 197
cybersurfing, 175, 176, 177

D

Dale, Dick, 76, 77, 79
Dana Point, Calif., 68, 69, 73, 155–156
Dewey Weber Surfboards, 111, 113
Doerner, Derrick, 180, 192
Dora, Mickey Chapin, 24, 82, 84, 85, 86–87, 113, 144
Dorian, Shane, 168, 170–171
Downing, George, 54, 60, 65, 192, 197
Drake, Jim, 142
drugs, 127, 129, 132

Duane, Daniel, 176
Dunne, Jessica, 188

E

Edwards, Phil, 25, 65, 68, 93, 94–95, 134
Endless Summer, The (film), 21, 24, 104, 109, 125, 192
Endless Summer II, The (film), 168
environmental awareness of surfers, 155–157
Evans, Bob, 92, 104, 106, 107

F

Fain, Johnny, 24, 82
Fantastic Plastic Machine, The (film), 108, 110
Farrelly, Midget, 104, 106, 107, 199–200
fashion. See clothing, surf-based
films, 41. *See also* surf films "beach," 73–74
Fitzpatrick, Jim, 82
Fletcher, Christian, 143, 162–163, 166, 167, 168
Foo, Mark, 178–179
Ford, Alexander Hume, 36
Freeman, Jim, 88, 89, 126
Freeth, George, 36, 37
Froiseth, Wally, 54, 60, 65, 197

G

Gidget (film), 69, 73, 74, 75
Gotcha Sportswear, 142, 161, 163, 164
Greenough, George, 93, 96, 107, 108, 112, 140
Griffin, Rick, 115, 129, 163, 188, 199
Grigg, Rick, 61, 97, 103

H

Hakman, Jeff, 129, 132, 133
Hamasaki, Joey, 153
Hamilton, Bill, 125, 140, 157
Hamilton, Gerry, 140
Hamilton, Laird, 176, 180, 181, 182–183, 192, 193
Hang-Ten, 96, 97, 162
Hawai'ian shirts, 61, 160–161
Hawai'ian surfing, 29–36, 37, 44, 94, 99, 103, 116, 118–119, 123, 124, 132, 133, 134, 136, 176, 177, 178
See also Makaha Beach, Hawai'i; O'ahu, Hawai'i; Waimea Bay, Hawai'i
competitions, 103
in early 1900s, 35
Hawai'ian culture and, 29–31, 33
introduction to California, 37
post-World War II, 59–63
in 1700s and 1800s, 30, 31, 33
in 1970s, 133, 136

Hemmings, Fred, 146, 150, 151, 153
Hening, Glenn, 158
Hermosa Beach, California, 68, 73
Hoffman, Joyce, 153
Hoffman, Walter, 60, 61
hollow boards, 44, 48
hot curl surfing, 54, 57, 59
"hotdog" surfers, 57, 82, 84
hotlines, surf, 193
Huntington Beach, Calif., 109, 140, 146–147
Hynson, Mike, 24, 103, 109, 120

I

Indonesia, 128
International Professional Surfers Association, 144, 151, 153
International Surfing (magazine), 92, 93
International Surfing Federation, 117, 150

J

Jacobs, Hap, 68
Jacobs Surfboards, 68, 111
Jarratt, Phil, 129
Jones, Malia, 152, 153

K

Kahanamoku, Duke, 37, 38, 40, 41, 45, 68, 110
Kalama, Dave, 180, 181, 192
Kanaiaupuni, Barry, 103, 119, 133
Kelly, John, 54
Kivlin, Matt, 82
Kohner, Frederick, 69, 74
Kohner, Kathy, 69, 74, 75
Kolsiana, Ralph, 79
Kwock, Danny, 142

L

language of surf culture, 33, 184, 188
Laverty, Bob, 128
Lawford, Peter, 55, 68
Leary, Dr. Timothy, 128, 200
leashes, 125
Lightning Bolt surfboards, 134, 164
Lindberg, Larry, 145
Liu, Mattie, 168, 170–171
London, Jack and Charmian, 29, 34, 35–36, 37
longboard, 144
    replacement of, 110, 111
    return of, 196, 197
Lopez, Gerry, 134–135, 136, 140, 149, 164, 176
Los Angeles Ladder Co., 44, 48
Lynch, Wayne, 112

M

McClelland, Hevs, 61
MacGillivray, Greg, 88, 89, 140
McKnight, Bob, 156
McTavish, Bob, 106, 107, 108
magazines, surfer images on, 175–176
magazines, surfing, 92–93, 97, 188, 193
Makaha Beach, Hawai'i, 60–61, 63
Maki, Clarence, 89
Malibu, California, 23, 24, 53, 55, 57, 58, 73, 74, 79, 80–81, 82, 123, 157
    beach movies and, 74, 75
    population increase, 82, 85, 88
    resistance to inland invaders, 85, 88
    small-wave surfing at, 84–85
Marcus, Ben, 178
Mearing, Kim, 153
media. *See* advertising; magazines, surf; surf films; surf music
Mexico, 129
Miggs, John, 160
migrations, surf, 60, 61
Milius, John, 137, 140
Moore, Bob, 68
Moorea, 70–71
Morey, Tom, 103, 104, 127
Morey (Tom) Invitational, 103–104, 144
Muñoz, Mickey, 63, 65, 73, 82, 96, 103–104, 161
museums, surf, 196
music. *See* surf music

N

Naish, Robby, 193, 194–195
National Scholastic Surfing Association, 144, 153
Naughton, Kevin, 126
Nazi imagery, 82
Nelson, Richard, 176
New Zealand, 130–131, 132
Noll, Greg, 61, 66–67, 67, 68, 73, 85, 88, 98, 99, 115, 193
nomadic explorations, 60, 61, 101, 125–26
North Shore. See O'ahu, Hawai'i
noseriding, 104, 196
nostalgia, surf, 175, 197
Nuuhiwa, David, 101, 103, 104, 107, 111, 113, 120, 150, 192

O

O'ahu, Hawai'i
    North Shore, 59, 60, 94, 99, 116, 123, 124, 132, 137, 140
Oberg, Margo Godfrey, 153, 154
O'Connell, Pat, 168
O'Donnell, Phyllis, 153
Ogden, Bill, 188
olo, 30, 193
Op sportswear, 163

Outrigger Canoe and Surfboard Club, 36, 37, 44, 45, 145–146
Owens, Bobby, 129

P

paddling, competitive, 44, 144
Palos Verdes Estates, California, 50–51, 65, 126
Patterson, Matt, 149
Pearl Jam, 156, 157, 159
Penuelas, Bob, 162, 163
Peruvian surfers, 29, 106
Peterson, Michael, 132
Peterson, Pete, 49, 53, 55, 79, 126
Pezman, Steve, 73, 128, 156, 175
photography, surf, 64, 65, 92–93, 96, 126
Pinsak, Dean, 129
Plastic Fantastic, 129
"pocket rockets," 111
Polynesia, 29, 32. See also Hawai'ian surfing
Pratte, Tom, 156–157, 158
professional surfing, 94–95, 96, 144, 146, 151, 153, 154, 164
Professional Surfing Association, 146
Propper, Gary, 99
psychedelic imagery, 111, 115, 129

Q

Quicksilver, 133, 142, 161, 163
Quicksilver Pro, 154, 156
Quigg, Joe, 55, 56, 71

R

Rasmussen, Rick, 132, 133
Raymond, Bruce, 136
Reichold Plastics, 68, 69
Renneker, Dr. Mark, 162
Richards, Mark, 164, 192
Rietveld, Rich, 161, 188
Rindge estate, 53, 55–56, 79
Rochlen, Dave, 55, 99
Rohloff, Grant, 89
Rosemberg, Tito, 126

S

San Onofre, Calif., 46–47, 48–49, 52, 53, 56
Santa Cruz Surfing Club, 66
Schwartz, Fred, 99
Schweitzer, Hoyle, 142
Scott, John, 144
seed culture, 29–37
Severson, John, 21, 88, 89, 90–91, 92–93, 97, 110, 115, 120, 129, 156, 180, 184, 188
Shank, Bud, 92
shark attacks, 173
shops, surfboard, 68, 69, 104, 167

shortboard revolution, 108, 111–113, 115–120, 196
Simmons, Robert Wilson, 56, 71, 88
skateboarding, 91, 92, 137, 142, 143, 160, 161, 162–163, 196
skysurfing, 196
Slater, Kelly, 156, 168, 170–171, 175–176, 176, 177
Slater, Sean, 168, 170–171
snowboarding, 142, 296
Solomon, Donnie, 178
Sorrell, Ron, 146
South Africa, 109, 123, 133, 151, 154, 196
Spreckels, Bunker, 116
Stewart, Mike, 127
stoke of surfing, 25, 198–209
   Hawai'ian culture and, 29–31
   surf films and, 64
Stoner, Ron, 132
strapsurfing, 176–177, 180, 192, 193, 196
Stüssy, Shawn, 142
surfboards, 24. See also specific brands or manufacturers
   advanced composite technology, 189
   auctions of, 189
   balsa chip boards, 56–57, 68, 69, 82
   Boogie Board, 104, 127, 196
   for collectors, 189, 193
   cost of, 189, 193
   design and material innovations, 24–25, 44, 48, 56–57, 103–104, 108, 111–113, 117, 127, 150, 189
   early Hawai'ian, 29, 30–31, 193
   fiberglass technology and, 56
   "gremmies," 68
   Hermosa Beach shops, 68
   Hobie, 69, 99
   hollow board, 44, 48
   "hot curl," 54
   "hotdog" surfing and, 57
   hydrodynamic, 56
   kneeboards, 112
   manufacturers of, 108
   "mini-gun," 111
   noserider, 104
   number sold annually, 167–168
   Plastic Machine, 108
   polyurethane foam, 68, 69
   psychedelic, 117
   Quigg balsa, 56
   shortboard revolution, 107–108, 110, 111–113, 115–120
   shot-cords (leashes), 125
   Simmons redwood, 56
   at Surf Line Hawai'i, 99
   Three-Fin Thruster, 143, 144, 197
   underground shapers, 112, 113
surfboard shops, 188, 189surf clubs, 103, 108, 120

surf culture, 25
   aspects of, 43
   author's entry into, 23–24
   beach movies and, 69, 73–76
   as big business, 113
   books about, 176
   change in, with shortboard, 111–112
   charisma of, 25, 113
   cult status of, 82, 162–163
   explosion into mainstream, 69, 73–81
   influence on contemporary life, 175–178, 180
   language of, 33, 184, 188
   mainstream media's portrayal of, 82
   media and, 93, 97
   as pop culture in 1990s, 161–162, 163, 167–168
   in postpsychedelic 1970s, 113
   seed culture, 29–37
   stoke at center of, 200
   surfing the Web, 175, 176, 177
   surf music and, 76–79
   surf Nazis and, 82
   transition to "pop" culture, 24
   versus beach culture, 175
Surfer (magazine), 21, 73, 82, 84, 92, 93, 97, 115, 132, 144, 146, 156, 178, 188, 200
surfer look, 160–161
surfers
   genuine, 199
   as nomads, 60, 61, 101, 125–26
   number in U.S., in 1997, 167–168
   public image of, 82, 199
Surfer's Journal, The (magazine), 54, 168, 175, 197
Surfer's Medical Association, 162
surf films, 64–65, 85, 88–89, 89, 92, 93, 104, 109, 112–113, 120, 126, 129, 134, 137, 140, 141, 162, 168
surfing
   essence of, 27
   as metaphor for life, 175
   modern, birth of, 37, 41
   resurgence in 1980s, 161
   spinoffs, 196
   state of the art, 189, 193, 197
   stoke of, 25, 198–209
surfing culture. See surf culture
Surfing (magazine), 163, 164
surfing magazines, 93, 193
Surf International (magazine), 93
Surfline, 134
surf music, 74, 76–79, 112, 120, 159, 193, 196
surf photography. See photography, surf
Surfrider Foundation, 156, 157, 158–159
surf spots, 122–123
Sutherland, Jock, 99, 103, 134, 136

T

Thomas N. Rogers Company, 44, 48
Tomson, Michael, 142
tow-in surfing. See strapsurfing
Townend, Peter, 136, 140, 144, 151
Tracks (magazine), 92, 93
trade shows, 97
Trent, Buzzy, 103
Twain, Mark, 33, 35

V

Valentine, Val, 89
Valiere, Steve, 186, 187
Van Artsdalen, Butch, 103, 134
Van Dyke, Fred, 61, 65, 103, 145–146, 151
Vedder, Eddie, 156, 157, 159
Velzy, Dale, 56, 57, 68, 69, 88, 103, 117, 189, 193
vocabulary of surf culture, 33, 184

W

Wahine, 188
Waikiki, Hawai'i, 29, 35, 37, 38, 41, 44, 54, 65
Waimea Bay, Hawai'I, 59, 61, 63, 66–67, 85, 99, 106, 123, 137, 178, 182–183
Warren, Mark, 136
WaveTrak International, 193
Weaver, Robert, 168
Web, surfing, 175, 176, 177
Weber, Dewey, 24, 111–112, 113
Websites on surfing, 177
Webster, Dale, 199
West, Jerry, 97
Western Surfing Association, 157
wetsuits, 142, 161, 167, 168
"Wilbur Kookmeyer," 162, 163
Wilson, Malcolm, 197
windsurfing, 142, 176, 192, 194–195, 196
Witzig, John, 93, 108, 112, 117
women surfers, 61, 91, 92, 103, 152, 153, 154, 155, 188
World Contest, 23, 101, 103, 121
World Surfing Championship, 106, 107, 113, 121, 150, 154
World War II, 56, 58

Y

Young, Nat, 12, 104, 106, 107, 108, 110, 111–112, 118, 144–145, 150, 157, 163, 196
Young, Robert "Nat", 104, 106

Z

Zahn, Tom, 53, 56, 59, 68, 74, 76, 79
Zamba, Frieda, 154